Jon Benzinger is a faithful p̷ is gifted at discerning the ti sightful preacher with his fir ing in the world. This means that he has something vitally important to say in this book. What is more, he has something that you need to hear. This book is critically important for the hour in which we live. Please read this book and you will greatly benefit from the truth found within it.

Steven J. Lawson
President, OnePassion Ministries

I've long considered my friend Jon Benzinger to be one of the most gifted expositors in the evangelical church today. So it is no surprise to me that he brings that same giftedness to *Stand: Christianity vs. Social Justice*. In this work, Jon meticulously lays out the historical and contemporary shortcomings of the social justice movement against the sufficiency and efficacy of the gospel. I am dogmatic in the belief that every Christian is an apologist (1 Pet 3:15). This book will help equip you to give a biblical defense against one of the most ungodly ideologies to come against the church in many decades.

Darrell B. Harrison
Dean of Social Media, Grace to You
Co-Host, the Just Thinking Podcast

Very rarely does a polemic radiate with a pastor's heart like this book does. Pastor Jon deals head-on with the problems with the current push for social justice with theological accuracy, biblical fidelity ,and true concern for Jesus's bride, the church.

Kofi Adu-Boahen
Pastor, Redeemer Bible Fellowship, Medford, OR

It is tragically far too rare these days for a pastor to so directly confront a widespread cultural lie. In this book, however, Jon Benzinger takes on a movement causing confusion and breaking relationships. He does so biblically and graciously, with courage and pastoral kindness. I'm grateful for this very important resource.

John Stonestreet
President, the Colson Center
Host, the BreakPoint podcast

One of the most insidious and destructive movements to sweep across both culture and Christianity in the last ten years has been the Social Justice Movement. In order to appeal to Christians, the movement has hijacked biblical language in order to present itself as orthodox. However, Social Justice is all law and no gospel. It is counterfeit. It is heresy. Yet seemingly few have had the courage and temerity to stand up to it. That's why I'm thankful for my friend, Jon Benzinger. Not only does *Stand* skillfully and biblically assess the tenets of the Social Justice Movement, but Jon also writes with godliness, humility, and lovingkindness. This is a much-needed book!

Nate Pickowicz
Teaching Pastor, Harvest Baptist Church, Gilmanton Iron Works, NH

A must-read for every Christian! Benzinger reaches into the academic hallway, grabs Social Justice, and pulls it down to be confronted by the Word of God. Truly an invaluable tool in the belt of every churchman.

Anthony Wood
Pastor-Teacher, Mission Bible Church

Almost one hundred years ago J. Gresham Machen published a clarion call that pitted Christianity against theological liberalism. As Machen saw it, there was no way an ideology so counter to Scripture's clear teaching could ever be confused with biblical Christianity; in fact, they were two entirely different religions. In our day, Jon Benzinger has done something similar. He has sounded the call and given the church a vital resource that demonstrates the Social Justice Movement (SJM) is not Christianity. Written with refreshing accessibility, *Stand* persuasively demonstrates that despite claims to the contrary, SJM distorts biblical justice by clothing it in neo-Marxist garb. The result is, as Dr. Benzinger argues, "a different gospel" much like what Paul refuted in Galatians. This brief book packs a huge punch!

Cory M. Marsh

Professor of New Testament, Southern California Seminary

Author, *A Primer on Biblical Literacy*

"They arrived confused, hurt, angry, or dejected, and all said the same thing, 'I lost my church to social justice'" (*Stand*, 4). My wife and I were attending and serving in one of those local churches for twenty-seven years when they opened their doors to the SJM. Over the course of the next six months, after exiting the church, I spoke with and met with dozens of people that were experiencing exactly what Jon saw and heard. When Jon preached and taught through the series that spawned this book, I witnessed the healing and clarity that was brought to hundreds of wounded saints. I am deeply humbled and abundantly privileged to sit under and stand beside Jon and the shepherds at RBC as they contend for and live out the gospel of our Lord Jesus Christ. My particular sphere of influence is the incarcerated within the state and federal prisons throughout our country. This book will be circulating within this mission field for decades to come.

Chuck Holmes

Founder/Director, Mt. Nebo Prison Ministry

As someone responsible for educating the next generation, I see the war that is being fought for the hearts and minds of today's youth. If you are a parent, then you need to read this book so you can be discerning regarding how your child's worldview is being shaped at school, through social media and at your church. The Social Justice Movement is everywhere, and this book will equip you to understand what it is and why it truly is a "different gospel." Once you have read it, your next responsibility is to get it in the hands of your pastor to protect your church from these heretical ideas. It's time for you to take a *Stand*.

Jim Desmarchais
Superintendent, Gilbert Christian Schools

Jon Benzinger writes with a shepherd's heart and wields a shepherd's rod, fiercely protective of his flock. These are the best kinds of books and resources, ones that flow from the trenches of local church ministry. Benzinger suggests that the SJM is the Galatian heresy of the twenty-first century. This book is a warning and a corrective to a false gospel that mixes faith and works, a false gospel that offers a fraudulent redemption and false hope. What happens in the west ultimately trickles out around the globe. Missionaries carry their beliefs and culture when they leave the USA for missionary work. *Stand* is written to inform, warn, and equip the people in your local church to stand against the false doctrine of the SJM—it is a volume I urge you to place in their hands.

Philip S. Hunt
Pastor, Kitwe Church, Kitwe, Zambia
Vice-Chancellor, Central Africa Baptist University

Discernment has historically been recognized as the ability to judge between that which is true and false. However, practically speaking, discernment is rightly understood as the ability to judge between that which is not only true and false, but between that which is true, almost true, and false. Nothing illustrates this truism of discernment better than the explosion of Social Justice throughout evangelicalism. Jon Benzinger's book, *Christianity vs. Social Justice*, offers biblical discernment into this most pressing heresy facing the evangelical church. Heresy? Why yes, because if one adopts the categories of Social Justice, they are fundamentally undermining the biblical understanding of Christianity. In short, a rose by any other name is still a rose; and a false understanding of Christianity by any other name is still a rank heresy.

William C. Roach
Director of Theological Studies, Veritas International University
Author, *Defending Inerrancy*.

Social Justice. Critical Race Theory. Wokeness. If these words leave you feeling uncomfortable or confused, you're not alone. They represent a seismic shift shaking our society to its core, and biblical Christianity is in its crosshairs. Every believer needs to understand a philosophy that is invading schools, offices, churches, media, and every other aspect of modern life. But how does one go about gaining that understanding? My friend, Dr. Jon Benzinger, provides the answer in his new book, *Stand*. Using the Book of Galatians, Jon lays bare the flawed foundational underpinnings of the Social Justice Movement. More importantly, he guides the reader through a solid biblical evaluation of the movement in a way that equips followers of Christ to stand firm in their faith and expose the movement's theological and doctrinal errors. This book is short, but it's "calorie rich" in terms of solid biblical teaching. Read it with a pen and notebook nearby, and pause at the end of each chapter to reflect on the study questions. Then when you're done, purchase several additional copies to share with friends and family. This book needs to be read by everyone follower of Jesus who is serious about being a witness for the truth in our day.

Charles Dyer
Professor-at-Large, Bible at Moody Bible Institute
Host, The Land and the Book radio program

There are many new books written to address the woke movement, but this is probably my favorite. Its short size makes it accessible to more readers. Its pastoral tone avoids needless offense. Its courage means it's not a back door entryway for woke third-way-ers to regain access to the precious Bride of Christ. It's also written by a pastor to average people, so it's not overly academic and lofty in its terminology. I am genuinely thrilled to endorse this book by my friend Jon Benzinger, and I'm eager to offer it to my congregation as a valuable resource to help them *Stand*.

Andy Woodard
Pastor, Providence Baptist Church, NY, New York
Founder, NonConformist Ministries

As culture has embraced Critical Social Justice (CSJ), many church leaders have capitulated on this issue. What we need in this hour are more men willing to *Stand* for the truth without concern for the consequences. Anyone familiar with Jon Benzinger can appreciate his strong *Stand* for truth while aptly demonstrating a pastoral heart of compassion for others. While Jon does not seek attention by racing into the latest cultural controversy, he's unflinching in his approach when an issue arises. Those around Jon benefit as his response is always thoughtful, measured, and by all means biblical. Pastors, lay leaders, and business professionals will appreciate the biblical lens he uses on the most controversial subject of our time. Jon's book, *Stand* is a must-have for anyone desiring the peaceful truth of God's Word rather than the culture's hostility.

Virgil Walker
Executive Director of Operations, G3 Ministries
Co-Host, the Just Thinking Podcast

Clarifying and digestible, but more importantly loving and firm. Stand presents a clear, concise case for taking a principled stand against "Social Justice" and for true justice, framed in the biblical understanding of justice that serves as the philosophical basis for the West. Highly recommended.

James Lindsay
Founder, New Discourses

Stand provides us a plain-spoken and persuasive case against the conceits of "social justice," which is, in fact, anti-social (nurturing perpetual, destructive resentment) injustice (hostile to impartiality and other cognate virtues). Though bold and pointed in his critique, Benzinger shuns a no-holds-barred approach, for he takes pains to bind himself to the essential protocols of biblical fidelity, rational discourse, and both tough and tender love. And for those who want to press on in this study, the bibliography is choice and extensive.

Mark Coppenger
Retired Professor of Christian Philosophy and Ethics,
Southern Baptist Theological Seminary

J.G. Machen knew that Liberalism in the 1920s had no good news. It was all "law." "Do." "Do more." One could never do enough. In the same vein, the Social Justice movement must never be called, "The Social Justice Gospel," because it is not good news nor does it proclaim good news. It is all law. It is "do." "Do more." Jon Benzinger rightly recognizes the vacuous nature of Social Justice and wisely titles the book, *Stand: Christianity vs Social Justice*. Social Justice is against Christianity and vice versa. The "vs" in the title is significant. The life, death, burial, resurrection, ascension, and intercession of Jesus Christ mean something. Jesus, grace incarnate, is alive and life giving. On its best day, Social Justice is dead, life taking. Social Justice divides, destroys, angers, and inflames. It is one thing when mass media, businesses, and universities extol Social Justice/CRT/Marxist ideologies. It is quite another when the church echoes the world with an eerily similar and incessant drumbeat. The churches' external enemies tend to unify the churches. On the other hand, internal enemies are the most problematic. They camouflage themselves and utilize Christian verbiage, all the while looking to devour Christ's sheep.

Thankfully, the Lord uses men of God to apply biblical tourniquets where necessary and administer spiritual CPR. One of those brave men is Jon Benzinger. By God's grace, Jon has been uniquely qualified to both biblically assess the state of Evangelical affairs and to offer the remedy and gospel-oriented hope. *Stand* needs to be in the hands of Christians, both leaders and lay people, so that they will be equipped to navigate the hostile landscape of the bad news of Social Justice.

Mike Abendroth
Pastor, Bethlehem Bible Church, West Boylston, MA
Host, No Compromise Radio

In this critical hour when Christians need a bulwark of truth and sound doctrine to help them withstand the insidious tsunami of social justice thinking that is flooding into many local churches, Jon Benzinger's book is a resource that will equip you to both understand and combat the evils of the social justice movement. Benzinger clearly and succinctly exposes the deceptive and destructive nature of the SJM monster by shining the light of God's Word upon it. Benzinger then hits the SJM monster on the head with the hammer of the Word, throws it on its back to expose its dark underbelly, and with exegetical precision guts the SJM beast with the sword of the Spirit. *Stand* is a critical work for pastors and laymen alike for these sad times when churches are being torn apart by the demonic doctrines and Satanic lies that underpin the SJM. Read *Stand*. It will help you, your family, and your church "stand firm against the schemes of the devil" (Eph 6:10–13).

Jack Hughes
Pastor-Teacher, Anchor Bible Church, Lousiville, KY

Raging and Controversial issues require courage, clarity and conviction. Jon addresses the subject of social justice with all three. He is biblical and pastoral. Whether you agree or not with his conclusions, you cannot deny the simplicity and soundness of his reasoning and application of the gospel to the social issues of society. Take up and read and share with friends and family.

Chopo Mwanza
Pastor, Faith Baptist Church Riverside, Kitwe
Faculty, Central African Baptist University

Many of us in corporate America have experienced a recent in-doctrination of this Marxist-driven movement firsthand. After decades of companies investing in social good and training in sensitivity and equality, something has seriously changed. *Stand* offers the insights we need to understand all that we're seeing unfold. This is a new movement of race theory-fueled hatred and divisiveness and *Stand* offers us timely wisdom from a trusted shepherd's heart on how to live in this age. I can no longer view the SJM as a secondary issue or a cultural fad, and after reading this neither can you. Benzinger exposes it here for what it is; SJM really is a "severe evil" and "perversion of true justice" (*Stand* 27, 28). This movement, by their own definition, seeks to overthrow capitalism and Christianity. As *Stand* explores the contrast with biblical justice, the SJM is strategically aimed at tearing down our systems of education, economics, and most importantly the eternity of its disciples. I'm so grateful for Jon's contagious courage and biblical exposition, exhorting us to unite in hope and action. I am honored to join Jon, and others with steel spines, in the battle to reject the praise of man, to live for Jesus's approval, and stand for truth and gospel-rooted biblical justice.

Brian Johnson
Technology & CyberSecurity Executive
Digital Parenting Advocate, ProtectYoungHearts.com

Stand isn't just a call to action, it equips you for action. Jon's insightful work is thorough yet clear and a breath of fresh air. He takes a dense topic and boils it down to bite sized chunks, making it a joy to read. If you've been waiting for a clear summary of why the Social Justice movement is clearly unbiblical and what you should do about it, this is your book!

David M. Jordan
Senior Pastor, Grace Bible Church, Purcellville, VA

In *Stand: Christianity vs. Social Justice*, Jon Benzinger has produced a well-researched, but readable, critique of the unbiblical and harmful Social Justice Movement (SJM) and Critical Race Theories (CRT) that are negatively impacting the church and biblical theology. Benzinger, as a skillful Watchman-Pastor, faithfully and skillfully sounds the trumpet by fulfilling Titus 1:9 in the best possible way, by directly refuting the false gospel of the "Great Awokening" of SJM and CRT and by clearly teaching sound doctrine on the nature of true, biblical justice. If you are a Christian concerned about oppression, injustice, racism, and other moral ills that plague our culture and you desire biblical clarity, you should read Benzinger's book for clear, biblical thinking on the subject.

Kevin Lewis
Professor of Theology & Law, Talbot School of Theology
Biola University

The gospel is the target of the enemy and one of the current attacks is social justice. In the book, *Stand*, Jon Benzinger has done a fantastic job of explaining the social justice attack and demonstrating from God's Word how to preserve the purity of Justification by grace alone, through faith alone, in Christ alone.

Chris Charles Mueller
Teaching pastor, Faith Bible Church in Wildomar California
Adjunct Faculty, The Masters Seminary

The Social Justice Movement distorts biblical justice and undermines the gospel. In fact, the SJM has become a false gospel, twisting the Scriptures and mixing faith with works. While many pastors have downplayed this issue or insist that this is nothing more than a second-tier issue, Benzinger makes a clear case that the SJM is a deadly strategy that Satan is using to assault the true gospel. A war on truth is raging. This book provides pastors and people with a real-world guide to fighting the good fight of faith.

Costi W. Hinn
Teaching Pastor, Shepherd's House Bible Church, Chandler, AZ
President/Founder, For the Gospel

The Social Justice Movement was the early fringe and stealth, subversive for Wokism within Christianity. It is now the infamous and un-silent destroyer of churches and denominations. Wherever SJM influence looms large, the gospel is largely forgotten or unknown. Jon Benzinger's *Stand* is a must-read, no-nonsense primer for any pastor or Christian leader who thinks critically and takes this threat seriously. Only the unchanging truth of the gospel can defeat the radical subjectivism of the SJM and the Woke agenda.

Ryan Helfenbein
Executive Director, the Standing for Freedom Center
Liberty University

Jon captured in a concise way the cultural battle with Christianity and the Social Justice Movement. His thoughtful style to communicate has the reader glued to each page. A must read. Super references. A must for your library.

Wayne Tesch
Co-Founder, For the Children

Dr. Benzinger has done a great service for us in writing this book. It needed to be written. In the spirit of J. Gresham Machen's *Christianity and Liberalism*, Dr. Benzinger lays bare the unbiblical nature of the views before us. In their mildest forms they are unbiblical. In their extreme forms they are completely non-Christian—another gospel—a false gospel. Indeed, Ibram Kendi (Ibram Henry Rogers) rejects what he terms "savior theology," historic orthodox Christianity, and replaces it with "liberation theology." We need to see these views for what they are, and to that end Dr. Benzinger properly frames the issues and exposes the blurred thinking that dishonors and even denies our lord Jesus Christ. Dr. Benzinger provides a clarion call, and we must heed it. This book needs to be widely read.

Craig S Hawkins
Professor

The prophet Ezekiel depicts God searching throughout Israel for a man to build up the wall and stand in the gap before him for the land (Ezek 22:30). Jon Benzinger is such a man for the church in the twenty-first century. He has counted the cost and taken his stand against the Social Justice Movement and its frontal attack against the glories of the gospel of Jesus Christ. With biblical clarity, and authority this book exposes the errors of the Social Justice Movement, not in a spirit of hatred but in a spirit of love—a love for those who are being deceived by the evil one, and a love for the church to be adequately equipped for every good work. Every Christian pastor, parent, and church member who reads this book will be equipped to discern what true justice is and will find the strength to stand in the gap and give a defense for the hope that is in them, yet with gentleness and reverence.

Andy Woodfield
Lead Pastor, Hickman Community Church

Stand is a simple, clear, and urgent call to discernment and action, written with precision by a pastor whose grasp of the issue is expert level. Jon is like a health inspector who has come into the kitchen of a restaurant that's making everyone sick. He's followed his trained nose to the stench and found the source of bacteria that's beautifully plated and delivered by the world, but from the stove of Satan. Read and digest this instead to be nourished on the words of sound doctrine.

Justin Erickson
Lead Pastor, Desert Bible Church in Scottsdale, AZ

Jon Benzinger has explained in a dramatic and scholarly fashion the nature of the Social Justice Movement and its assault upon Christianity. I applaud his courage and stand with him on his challenge to the Christian church today to defend the truth whatever the cost may be. Here is an informative and very useful tool for the Christian to stand firm against the schemes of the devil and sin.

Alex Montoya
Senior Pastor, First Fundamental Bible Church, Whittier, CA

STAND

CHRISTIANITY VS SOCIAL JUSTICE

FOREWORD BY OWEN STRACHAN

JON BENZINGER

Stand: Christianity vs. Social Justice
Copyright © 2022 by Jon Benzinger

Published by G3 Press
4979 GA-5
Douglasville, GA 30135
www.G3Min.org

Printed in the United States of America by Graphic Response, Atlanta, GA.

ISBN: 979-8-9855187-3-3

Cover Design: Scott Schaller

To my children—Colin, Ava, Emma, and Jace—and the children of Redeemer Bible Church in Gilbert, Arizona. Faithfulness to Jesus in the decades you're growing up in requires much more self-discipline, wisdom, love, and courage than I probably needed when I was a kid. May books like this fortify your souls for all the battles you will face as followers of Jesus in these increasingly dark days.

CONTENTS

Acknowledgements i

Foreword iii

Introduction....................................... 1

PART 1: WHY SHOULD CHRISTIANS STAND AGAINST THE SOCIAL JUSTICE MOVEMENT?

1 A Generational Attack.........................9

2 The Cure That Kills The Patient...................... 13

3 True Justice vs. Social Justice, Part 1.................17

4 True Justice vs. Social Justice, Part 2 23

5 A Completely Different Religion......................29

PART 2: WHAT IF CHRISTIANS DON'T STAND AGAINST THE SOCIAL JUSTICE MOVEMENT?

6 A Darker Remake of the Failed Original......... 41

7 Four Truths That Fight Disunity....................49

8 An Oxymoronic Contradiction 55

PART 3: WHAT CAN CHRISTIANS DO TO STAND AGAINST THE SOCIAL JUSTICE MOVEMENT?

9 An Oasis in Our Lost and Dying World 65

10 The Bewitching is Real.................................... 73

11 Having a Steel Spine.................................... 81

Conclusion 89

Appendix 1: Recommended Resources 93

Appendix 2: What Black Lives Matter
    Believes...111

ACKNOWLEDGEMENTS

First and foremost, I want to acknowledge my wife Katie who told me to write this book nine months before Owen Strachan did. I ignored her and this is my public confession! I also want to thank Owen Strachan who I did listen to when he encouraged me to write this book. Without his friendship and belief that the content would honor God and help the Body of Christ, this would not be in your hands now.

Third, while I am grateful to Diana Nichol, David Mataya, Shawna Thackrah, and Jac Chen for reading a rough draft of this book and offering suggestions, I want to recognize especially Drs. Craig Hawkins and Mark Coppenger, who put a considerable amount of time and effort into helping me make sure that what I said here was accurate. Any mistakes should be understood as completely my fault.

Fourth, I want to honor the people of Redeemer Bible Church in Gilbert, Arizona, the church where I get to be one of the pastors, especially Pastors Dale Thackrah and Kyle Swanson. Your love, encouragement, gratitude, and willingness to share this material with those you care about helped me see just how important a work like this can be in the lives of God's people. Protecting you drove me to preach the series that was expanded into this book.

Fifth, this book would not exist if it wasn't for the pastors and professors who poured their lives and God's Word into mine. I am an accumulation of their collective impact on my life during my most formative years. Ron Wright especially, but also Wayne Tesch, George Wood, Jim Bradford, James Torres, Mike Fabarez, Craig Hawkins, Frank Beckwith, John MacArthur, Alex Montoya, Steve Lawson, and Dave Farnell—this book has your fingerprints all over it because my life always will.

Sixth, I cannot say "Thank you" enough to the men who lead G3 Ministries—Josh Buice, Virgil Walker, and Scott Aniol—for publishing this book. It is one of the kindest gestures anyone has ever done for me, making me forever grateful to these men for believing that this content will honor God and put steel in the spines of Christians all over the world.

Last and most importantly, I want to thank the Lord Jesus Christ, who will bring every word of this book into judgment (Matt 12:36–37). I hope and pray that it brings you glory (1 Cor 10:31), helps lost people come to know you (John 17:3), and encourages your people to love and serve you (Deut 10:12–13).

FOREWORD

The Bible is not a boring or tame book. It's actually pretty wild. It contains an epic war between good and evil, and this war unfolds through numerous dramatic face-offs between the people of God and the people of Satan. Moses before Pharoah; David against Goliath; Christ against Satan; and Elijah against 450 prophets of Baal. It was the worst of times, Elijah's day. Yet he did not go silent. He saw that the nation of Israel was being taken over by godlessness. He watched the people drift into idolatry. So, in God's providence, Elijah called a show-down between Baal's priests and himself. A conflict and confrontation for the ages, this was.

Two offerings would be prepared, one to Baal, and one to God. The people would have to choose their way depending on which being answered. This is what we hear Elijah saying in 1 Kings 18:21, a passage that echoes in our day:

> And Elijah came near to all the people and said, "How long will you go limping between two different opinions? If the LORD is God, follow him; but if Baal, then follow him." And the people did not answer him a word.

We know the rest of the story. The Baal-followers heard nothing from Baal, while fire fell from heaven as the Lord answered righteous Elijah. The truth won out that day. Elijah had taken his stand, and the Lord God vindicated him.

We are in no less a convulsive moment today. As Jon Benzinger's excellent short book *Stand* shows, we are in a time for standing. The false gospel of wokeness and social justice is advancing everywhere around us. Few know what is happening; fewer still speak against this godless ideology. Like a shadow creeping over a sunlit mountain pasture, Marxist social justice is now overtaking true biblical justice. People are being told they're complicit in "white supremacy" based not on their actions or words, but the color of their skin. The entire public order, we are told further, is infested with "systemic racism," a terrible poison that is at once everywhere and nowhere.

This sounds new, but it is not. It is the old "social gospel" with a software update. It is no gospel at all, but an anti-gospel. It teaches as Jon makes clear that minorities in our society are inherently and inescapably oppressed. Then, having diagnosed a false problem, it changes the good news of Christ to focus on so-cial liberation, not spiritual salvation. All must mobilize in this struggle for "social justice," or else suffer for their unwillingness. How confusing this is, for it is absolutely true that every believer must hate evil, and that our doctrine of justice—as Jon shows in spades—is rich and textured in extremity. True biblical justice fights evil, makes way for compassion, and collides head-on with ungodly systems like Marxism. (Marxism is history's most suc-cessful bad idea, having led to the deaths of some 100 million people globally).

But true biblical justice is not at all the same system as Marxist social justice. The two are incompatible, as Jon argues. Sadly, many evangelicals hear that this sort of clarity is unneces-sary; in a good number of cases, the sheep in fact do not want clarity, but ear-tickling words (2 Tim 4:3-4). Many today thus limp between two opinions, and actually think this is ideal. Bet-ter not to be right or left; better to play the middle, never choose sides, never act decisively. But thankfully, not every pastor or church or Christian takes this approach. Some men—with many believers across the world—still stand on God's Word. Some pas-tors call the people not to limp. They summon them to the solid rock of truth. This is what Jon does in *Stand*. It is not too much to say it this way, switching the metaphor: you have in your hands the antidote to the spirit of the age.

Whether you are a believer or not yet a Christian, I urge you: feast on this book. Read it slowly. Gather your family, or your college roommates, or even total strangers (!) as you read it. Vocalize paragraphs out loud, then discuss them. Watch as God uses this book to first help you see clearly, then help you strategize effectively, then help you go and bear witness. This is what the world needs: a flooding of all markets, all channels, with divine truth. You do this best, of course, when you stand with a body of believers, a local church that adores and proclaims sound doctrine.

The days are evil, and none of us knows what we have in store. But God's people are called in every age to emulate Elijah and stand. This is what Jon Benzinger has done. This is what his fellow pastors—and the church's members—at Redeemer Bible Church have done, with Kyle Swanson and Dale Thackrah in particular holding up their friend's arms as he wages war on the devil and his schemes (2 Cor 10:3-6). This now is what you must do. Whether you have been shepherded or not toward God's Word in the past, do not limp between two opinions for a moment longer. The hour is late; the time for choosing is upon us.

As you do so in Christian faith, know this: if Satan attacks you, if the outcome of your witness is not victory as in Elijah's day, God has you in his hands. You can take your own Elijah-like stand because you know that even if the forces of evil take you down, even if they destroy your reputation and dox you publicly, even if they disown you, even if they push you off the ledge, you will only fall into the everlasting arms. You are never alone, and you will be rewarded on the last day. As a Christian, you know what Elijah knew, and more: Christ will never let you go (John 10:28).

With this confidence, even as many have inexplicably gone mute and left the battlefield, let us not shrink back. Let us speak. Let us tell the truth. In love, let us preach the gospel. The Lord is God; let us follow him, come what may.

Dr. Owen Strachan
Provost, Grace Bible Theological Seminary
Author, *Christianity and Wokeness* and *Reenchanting Humanity*

If I profess with the loudest voice and clearest exposition every portion of the truth of God except precisely that little point which the world and the devil are at the moment attacking, I am not confessing Christ, however boldly I may be professing Christ. Where the battle rages, there the loyalty of the soldier is proved and to be steady on all the battle front besides, is mere flight and disgrace if he flinches at that point.[1]

---

[1] Attributed to Martin Luther. Quoted in Francis A. Schaeffer, *The Complete Works of Francis A. Schaeffer: A Christian Worldview*, vol. 4 (Westchester, IL: Crossway, 1982), 333.

INTRODUCTION

I should not have been the one to write this book.

For decades, evangelicals have had a class of watchmen (Ezek 33:1–7) who took up the mantle of protecting the church. Since God saved me in 1995, I have praised him many times for our protectors, praying often "Thank you, Lord, that so and so is on our side." For over two decades, I have seen them alert the faithful to such threats as the prosperity movement, pragmatism, postmodernism, feminism, open theism, the Emergent Church, the New Perspective on Paul, the New Atheism, and the homosexual agenda. These watchmen blew the trumpet, marshaled their theological firepower, and safeguarded the church courageously. As a result, they were trusted, revered, and celebrated as heroes that are valiant for the truth and valuable to emulate. One of them should have written this book. However, since the Social Justice Movement (SJM) started advancing within evangelicalism in the mid-2010s, our watchmen, except for a handful of brave exceptions, have been silent.

I have the honor of pastoring a church in Arizona called Redeemer Bible Church (redeemeraz.org). Doing so is one of the great joys of my life. If we are not careful, pastors can make the mistake of speaking outside of their area of expertise. Therefore, reader, I should let you know a little bit about me. When I was in college, I came to believe that I should prepare for pastoral ministry like a missionary prepares for the mission field. I thought I needed to understand both the Bible and my early twenty-first century American society. I wanted to do a good job of bridging the gap between my culture and biblical cultures. As a result, before entering seminary, I completed a master's degree with an emphasis on postmodern ideology and political philosophy at an evangelical law school. I studied theology and philosophy, logic and argumentation, legal and constitutional theories as well as cultural hot button issues like racism, euthanasia, pluralism, and abortion. In the course of study, I was exposed to the beliefs of some of the most influential postmodern theorists as well as both Christian and non-Christian critiques of their views.

Upon graduation, I taught as an adjunct professor for four years at a Christian university where my class offerings were Old and New Testament Survey, Christian Theology, Christian Worldview, and Church History, most of which I have also taught to pastors, missionaries, and laypeople overseas. Though far from being an expert, my education and experience have given me insights into the biblical and logical deficiencies of the SJM. Because of this, as early as 2015, when I saw InterVarsity publicly promoting the Black Lives Matter organization,[1] I thought, "If I can see the social justice assault on the truth, why aren't our watchmen fighting back yet? Well, don't worry. They will, eventually. I'll wait."

Expecting them to blow the trumpet and rally an assault on this ideology made me late to the game. For a short time, I thought to myself, "If our watchmen haven't responded, maybe it's not that big of a threat. If they aren't responding, maybe I'm wrong about it." However, it became clear to me that the SJM is, as I will seek to prove in the pages that follow, the most formidable threat to the gospel in our day. Then, as Christians began dividing, denominations battled, schools fractured, and churches split, I thought, "Our watchmen have to respond now. They will answer the call. The enemy is now inside our gates." As late as the height of the riots in the summer of 2020, I said to myself, "It's really past the time they should've responded, but surely, as cities burn, our watchmen will unite and go to war now." Nope. Crickets.

---

[1] Press Room, "InterVarsity and Black Lives Matter," *InterVarsity*, December 31, 2015, accessed January 17, 2021, https://intervarsity.org/news/ intervarsity-and-blacklivesmatter; Rod Dreher, "Do #UnbornLivesMatter To InterVarsity?," *The American Conservative*, January 8, 2016, accessed January 17, 2021, https://www.theamericanconservative.com/dreher/black-lives-matter-unborn-intervarsity-abortion.

Then, in the fall of 2020, two experiences thrust me into the fight. First, I attended *The Great Awokening* conference where it became obvious that the SJM was not a second-tier issue, but an actual attack on the gospel and biblical Christianity.[2] Second, people at Redeemer started sharing that they were suffering from the impact of the SJM. First, a mom came to me after church, tears in her eyes, saying, "My daughters, both home-schooled through high school, had one semester of college and they've not only rejected Christianity, but they're calling my husband and me 'privileged oppressors' because we're white." Another mom, again through tears, "My Thanksgiving will be ruined. My son is now woke and won't stop calling us racists." A third person, working in the field of education, warned me that the SJM had infiltrated Gilbert, Arizona and that Critical Race Theory (CRT) was being taught in our public schools. She said that some educators are "teaching our children that much of life and American history is racist, and so are they if they're white."[3] My friend recently confirmed this, telling me that his daughter dropped her Intercultural Communications class at our local junior college because it was social justice indoctrination and any dissent would get her removed from the class anyway. A fourth person talked to me about being forced to choose between her Christian convictions and her longtime job in the field of educational curriculum.

I could stay silent no longer. I had to do something. I had to make it clear that Redeemer would be a safe place to go to church. I could not wait for our watchmen any longer. I too was charged with being a watchman for the people entrusted to my care (Acts 20:28–31). A sermon series in November 2020 called *Stand: Christianity vs. Social Justice* was my response. Our church

---

[2] Sovereign Nations, "The Great Awokening Conference," *YouTube*, October 26, 2020, accessed October 31, 2020, https://www.youtube.com/playlist?list=PLZJe-MWy0cYcXTzIUVp8kK6gKRpNuck18.

[3] Gilbert, Arizona, the city Redeemer Bible Church is in, is 70% Caucasian according to "QuickFacts: Gilbert town, Arizona," *United States Census Bureau*, no date, accessed December 9, 2020, https://www.census.gov/quickfacts/ gilberttownarizona.

needed to see the SJM through a biblical lens and to understand how to relate to their 'woke' family members and friends with truth and love. Ultimately, three sermons, four interviews, and six podcasts (called *Redeeming Truth*, episodes #49–52, 54, and 57 [see also #24, #28, #74, and #78]) were the result. Most alarmingly, hundreds of people began showing up at Redeemer after the *Stand* series from a handful of churches in our area. They had publicly advocated social justice dogma while naively trying to integrate it with Christian theology. Dozens came to us for help. They arrived confused, hurt, angry, or dejected, and all said the same thing, "I lost my church to social justice."

Though I am aware I could be mercilessly criticized for this volume, it is my obligation as a pastor to refute dangerous ideology (2 Tim 2:24–26, Titus 1:9) in a way that helps others do the same (Eph 4:11–12) while not being disrespectful or hateful (1 Pet 3:15). The following pages were written to accomplish these goals. I also wrote this book to be accessible to everyone. If you find that I used words and concepts without defining them well, you can look them up in the indispensable and devastating Social Justice Encyclopedia on the New Discourses website or in the back of Owen Strachan's excellent book, *Christianity and Wokeness*. These resources will help you understand what the SJM really means by what it says. Also, if you want to dig deeper (which you should!), see the extensive recommended resources list in appendix 1. Many of the courageous exceptions to the silent watchmen have their books, videos, and websites listed there. My one suggestion for reading *Stand* is to do so with an open Bible. That way you can look up all the references as you make your way through each section. I've also created study questions after each chapter to aid the learning process.

The most common feedback I've received for this material has been, "I knew there was something wrong with the Social Justice Movement, but I didn't know exactly what to say. You gave me the words I need to understand it and to explain why it's unbiblical to my friends and family." That is my hope for you too! As you read the following pages, I will have succeeded if you see why the only right response to the SJM is to stand against it and to show others why they must do the same.

PART 1

WHY SHOULD CHRISTIANS STAND AGAINST THE SOCIAL JUSTICE MOVEMENT?

A GENERATIONAL ATTACK

The Christians in Galatia were facing a threat unlike anything the early church had faced up to that point and they did not know it. The issues raised in these churches were the same issues that led to the first church council (Acts 15), but sad to say, many of the same issues are still with us to this day. We learn from Paul's letter to the Galatian churches that the gospel can be attacked and Christians can miss it. We see that those who assault it will often use portions of the Bible as a weapon against sound doctrine. They may even twist the meaning of the Bible to fit an unbiblical agenda. We realize from the letter that those who attack the gospel may well believe they are promoting it when they are actually undermining it. We also learn that those who threaten the gospel can be some of the most prominent Christian leaders we have. Most importantly, it is clear that any addition to, subtraction from, or modification of the gospel nullifies its saving effects. If the attack on the gospel in Galatia had not been thoroughly refuted, it would have split the church in its infancy.

Every generation has unique attacks on the gospel to confront. Some are obvious, such as through your obedience you can earn heaven or become the god of your own world. However, most attacks are subtle. They are so subtle that many confessing Christians, even leaders, fail to notice the assault and follow lies. In the early centuries of the church, the attacks centered on who Jesus is and what He did. During the Protestant Reformation, the Reformers were raised up to defend the truth that salvation is by grace alone (not grace and merit), through faith alone (not faith plus works), and in Christ alone (not Jesus and the Church). For the last couple hundred years, Christians have been in a battle for the Bible that's still raging. The attacks come and go, but one thing seems certain, the attacks will not cease until Jesus returns.

The church of Jesus Christ around the world today is facing a generational challenge to the gospel that echoes the Galatian crisis in many key ways. The Christians promoting this attack believe, some of them with all their heart, that they are promoting the gospel when what they're doing is using the Bible to weaken its message. Some of the most prominent leaders in the evangelical Christian world are either helping to advance this assault or remaining silent while we wait and wait and wait for them to wake up and be allies in the fight. Some are far too sophisticated to call what we are facing an attack. Instead, they rush to find a middle ground, a third way that ultimately mixes truth with error while sounding quite sophisticated and trying to avoid looking like an alarmist or an extremist.

Evangelical leaders are doing this because they are either dominated by the fear of man (a temptation evangelicals have regularly succumbed to throughout history), do not have the tools to understand the issues adequately, or blindly parrot the ideas of a favorite teacher who was trusted in the past, but should not be trusted now. Many are talking about things from a position of authority they simply do not have the training to understand. Others know better and should be ashamed of themselves. In an effort to believe the best, I think many Christians are well-meaning. However, their superficial knowledge of the current attack has introduced poison into the body of Christ that is weakening our message and confusing our mission. If this does not stop soon, this poison will keep on splitting schools, churches, denominations, friendships, and families. All of this and more (as you'll see in coming chapters) potentially makes this onslaught against the truth the greatest threat to the church today.

Why would I say that so boldly? How do I know this will happen? A similar attack already had these disastrous effects about a hundred years ago (more about that in Part 2). Think about it, many who were together for the gospel for over a decade are now at odds, but it wasn't creationism that tore them apart. It wasn't spiritual gifts. It wasn't church governance. It wasn't baptism. It wasn't eschatology. It was one specific assault on the truth, originating from outside of Christianity, that ended their unity and put once close friends on opposite sides of this conflict.

What is this attack on the gospel? What is being promoted by many who think they're being faithful to the gospel when, in fact, they're not? What attack is using the Bible to undermine the gospel? What assault is being advanced thanks to the activity, inactivity, or silence of prominent and trusted Christian leaders? What challenge, if not thoroughly refuted, will continue to end decades of unity and faithfulness to the gospel? This attack on the church of Jesus Christ is the Social Justice Movement (SJM)[1] especially as it relates to ethnicity, but also as it includes gender and sexual preference. This three-headed, social justice monster,[2] just like the Galatian heresy, will decimate true Christianity unless, like Paul, faithful Christians take a stand.

STUDY QUESTIONS

1. List the attacks against the gospel that you've seen during your time as a Christian.

2. What were some of the ways that God used courageous people to fight those attacks?

3. Read Galatians 1:6–9. What specific words does Paul use to describe and what specific responses does Paul model to the message of the false teachers attacking the Galatian churches of his day?

---

[1] Also known as Critical Social Justice and promoted in programs like Social and Emotional Learning.

[2] Unbeknownst to me when I preached the series in 2020, back in 2019, Josh Buice called the SJM a "three-headed dragon" in this excellent article, "Why is Social Justice the Biggest Threat to the Church in the Last One Hundred Years?," *Delivered By Grace*, April 4, 2019, accessed December 21, 2021, https://g3min.org/social-justice-biggest-threat/.

THE CURE THAT KILLS THE PATIENT

The SJM is not Christianity. The message, the methods, the mission, the desired outcomes are not Christian. It is an anti-Christian philosophy disguised as truth and love that has captured much of the visible church. Like a virus, it is a foreign antibody injected into the body of Christ. The SJM, utilizing the philosophy of Critical Theory and Intersectionality, is poisoning the church, spreading strife, and attacking the very heart of the gospel. This book comes from a burden I have to care for God's people and teach them the truth. I want to protect them from a dangerous ideology that is infiltrating the Bible-believing, gospel-promoting churches and other institutions. This battle, however, is not just for pastors, theologians, and professors. It is a fight that must engage every Christian because the fight is coming for every Christian. No one is safe from the attack; therefore, no one has the luxury of sitting this one out.

Just to be clear, nothing said in this book is written with the goal of advancing racism, sexism, or classism, or advocating that those things either don't exist or are not still problems around the world and in Christian churches. We should listen to and love our neighbors who differ from us and have different experiences than we do even while adamantly disagreeing with their interpretation of their experiences.[1] Just because a person feels oppressed does not mean they actually are. There can be a difference between our feelings and reality—every parent knows this! We should care for the poor (Gal 2:10), address oppression (Isa 1:17), and weep with those who weep (Rom 12:15). The sins of one generation can have deep effects on the next. Obviously, there

---

[1] Norman Geisler, *Christian Apologetics* (Grand Rapids: Baker Books, 1976), 77–80.

are injustices in the world. Our society, our culture, our governments, and our churches are filled with sinners, and sinful people create injustices, which they then impose on other people. Humans have done this since Genesis! People have been murdered and abused, marginalized and silenced, forgotten and discriminated against—no doubt! Wherever there's been injustice, justice should be served. Wherever there is oppression it should be stopped. We should evangelize the lost and work to fix wrongs in our society, "so that in everything you [Christians] may adorn the doctrine of God our Savior" (Titus 2:10).

All that being said, the SJM does not and cannot diagnose any of these problems correctly, whether in the church or the culture. Just listen to what they espouse: "All people fall into one of only two categories: oppressors and oppressed." "Racism, sexism, homophobia, and transphobia are ordinary, built in to and impacting all of our thoughts about people as well as all of society's institutions and explain all disparities between groups." "All white people are racists." "All men are sexist and benefit from the patriarchy." "Racism is the unequal allocation of privilege based on race, not hatred based on race." "Social justice is about taking privilege from oppressor groups (i.e., white, heterosexual males) and redistributing it to oppressed groups." "Jesus was a political revolutionary, here to liberate the oppressed." "Salvation is more corporate, freeing people from oppression, than it is individual, freeing individuals from sin, death, and hell." "White, heterosexual males are unequally privileged whether they know it or like it or not." "All white people are complicit in the perpetuation of white supremacy and systemic racial injustice." "White people are discriminating against people of color all the time without being aware of it." "Society is systemically oppressive in its benefitting of white people, men, and heterosxuals." "In all human interactions, the question is not was there racism, but how did racism manifest itself." "There are only racists and anti-racists." "Men and white people have an unconscious bias against women and people of color." "Men, whites, and heterosexuals are too fragile to confront their privilege." "All progress from the Civil Rights Movement is a myth." "White supremacy is not about hate groups, but the cultural dominance of white people." "Any race can suffer from whiteness if they align themselves with white supremacy." "Diversity, equity, and inclusion (often combined and abbreviated DEI) is how we should address society's oppression." "Gender is non-binary." "There are 72 genders." "There are 78 gender pronouns." "LGBT people are discriminated against when we assume that most people are heterosexual." "We need to create safe spaces for women and people of color that are free from the white or male gaze." "Only women and people of color, because of their lived experience within a sexist and racist culture, can have knowledge of oppression." And my personal favorite, "Dear God, please help me to hate white people."[2]

Ideologies that believe these kinds of things will only increase poverty, injustice, oppression, discrimination, and marginalization, and do so exponentially while myths like systemic oppression, the patriarchy, white fragility, and the like fuel their cause. It cannot fix any real problems. It will only make them worse. It is the experimental cure that kills the patient, the patient being the countries of the world, including America, and the evangelical church. It is another gospel that will save no one from God's wrath, but will create rival churches. It should never be integrated with Christianity. It should be exposed and erased from Christianity as soon as possible.

As the following pages endeavor to show, the SJM is the latest attempt (and probably the most successful to date) to popularize postmodern ideologies and champion atheistic political philosophies. This makes the SJM "a different gospel" on the same level as the soul-damning heresy Paul refuted in Galatians. It is "contrary" to the gospel because it "distorts" the gospel, making it "another" gospel altogether (Gal 1:6–9).

---

[2] Nicole Fallert, "'Help Me Hate White People': Entry in Bestselling Prayer Book Stokes Controversy," *Newsweek*, April 8, 2021, accessed May 3, 2021, https://www.newsweek.com/help-me-hate-white-people-entry-bestselling-prayer-book-stokes-controversy-1582043.

Now, I know these are very lofty statements. In what follows, I intend to prove them all.

STUDY QUESTIONS

1. Read Galatians 1 and 2 carefully. Is it possible for trusted Christian leaders to be influenced by heretical teachings for a time? Explain your answer using what you just read in Galatians.

2. In light of what you just read from Galatians 1 and 2, how are Christians supposed to respond when trusted Christian leaders are influenced by heretical teachings?

3. Read Titus 2:10. According to this text, what is the effect of our good works on those who watch our lives? Why is this important?

TRUE JUSTICE VS. SOCIAL JUSTICE, PART 1

There are at least two reasons why the SJM is a distortion of the gospel: 1) The SJM misunderstands justice, and because of that, 2) it substitutes the true gospel for a false one. The teachings of the SJM are not in the same category as secondary issues like the timing of the Rapture or the continuation of miraculous spiritual gifts—doctrines that Christians disagree on. Regardless of our views on these secondary issues, we will be in heaven together. Those who believe the core teachings of the SJM contradict the essential teachings of the only message of hope in the world, the gospel of Jesus Christ. How exactly does it do that? How does the SJM misunderstand justice? To answer these questions, we must be clear on what the Bible says about justice. As we do, the social justice misunderstanding of justice and its subsequent distortion of the gospel will become obvious.

To start, there is no gospel ("good news") of Jesus's death and resurrection without bad news, and the bad news begins with the fact that God exists (Gen 1:1, Exod 3:14). He created everything, including you (Neh 9:6), which means he owns you (Ps 24:1–2, Ezek 18:4). This God is also holy (Lev 11:44–45), which includes his purity (Hab 1:13, 1 John 1:5), his hatred for sin (Zech 8:17, Heb 1:9), his goodness (Ps 100:5), and his justice (Deut 32:4, Ezra 9:15). As holy, he must and will punish all sin since it is right and good for him to do so (Ps 9:7–8, Isa 13:11, Acts 17:31, Rom 2:12).

"Righteousness and justice are the foundation of his throne" (Ps 97:2). God's rule as King over his universe includes dispensing what is deserved. When he gives people what they deserve, he is only doing what is right, which is exceedingly bad news for sinners like us. Compare your life to the Ten Commandments (Exodus 20:1–20) and there is no doubt about your guilt before

God. Because there is no justice without also doing what is right, and God's Word defines what is right, and God only does what is right (Dan 4:37), then it must be part of his good nature to punish those who are guilty of defying his Word (Exod 34:7, Nah 1:3). All injustice—like letting the guilty go unpunished or punishing the innocent—is, therefore, unrighteous, evil, and against God's character (2 Chr 19:7, Zeph 3:5, Rom 9:14). As an aside, any worldview that denies monotheism will always have an issue with justice because there is nothing above humanity for people to be accountable to.

Because God is just (Deut 32:4) and perfectly practices justice (Dan 4:37), he requires that his people practice justice as well (Ps 82:3, 112:5; Mic 6:8). Now, while it may seem that social justice is actual justice, as John Stonestreet, the President of the Colson Center, once said to me on our *Redeeming Truth* podcast, "It's no good having the same vocabulary if we're using different dictionaries." The phrase *social justice* has nothing at all to do with true justice. It conveniently dodges definition. The phrase is used to excuse injustice while hiding behind the word *justice* and redefining what it actually is. Practically speaking, it ends up meaning whatever political change progressives (i.e., socialists) support. In contrast to the dogma of the SJM, there are at least six marks of true justice:

First, justice in the Bible is marked by *compassion*. While compassion is not equivalent to justice, compassion for victims drives the need for justice. Justice provides closure for those who have been wronged. It is a public recognition that they were victims of something they did not deserve and the community stands with them and against the perpetrator. Justice served becomes a compassionate proclamation that as a society we care about the wrongs people suffer. Injustice is not compassionate because it callously dismisses the suffering of real victims.

Additionally, in Titus 3:4, God is described with the phrase "loving-kindness," which translates the Greek *philanthropia*, a word that means a lover of humanity. It refers to someone eager to alleviate pain, trouble, or danger. The context of Titus 3 is salvation from God's wrath for human sin. So, God, being moved with compassion, came up with an ingenious plan for humanity to escape his wrath (cf. John 3:16). He rescues sinners from his own accurate and appropriate judgment while remaining perfectly just at the same time. He did not do this by simply ignoring our sin—that would be unjust! Instead, God remains just and satisfies his justice while mercifully declaring sinners right with him (Rom 3:21-31), and he did so by taking that justice upon himself. Jesus, the sinless Son of God, the Second Person of the Trinity (John 1:1, 14; Col 2:9, Titus 2:13), died in the place of sinners, willingly and even joyfully receiving the justice we deserve (Mark 15:33-39, Heb 12:2). For anyone who believes in Jesus and repents of his rebellion, God will show him mercy and save him from his just, good, and right punishment for his sins (John 3:18, 36; Acts 11:18, 20:21; Rom 10:9-10, Eph 2:8-9).

Then, as people who have experienced God's compassion instead of his justice, Christianss should move towards others in compassion to help meet their needs (1 John 4:10-11). The Apostle John, Jesus's closest friend and the last surviving apostle, describes this responsibility for Christians with

> By this we know love, that he laid down his life for us, and we ought to lay down our lives for the brothers. But if anyone has the world's goods and sees his brother in need, yet closes his heart against him, how does God's love abide in him? Little children, let us not love in word or talk but in deed and in truth. (1 John 3:16-18)

Because God has been merciful to us, we should work to meet the needs of the poor and the suffering, especially other Christians (Deut 24:12-15, Prov 31:9, Isa 10:1-2, Jas 2:15-16). These texts focus on individuals (not governments!) who have the means to help those without. People with means who don't help those with needs are harshly spoken to in the Bible (Deut 15:7-11, Jas 5:1-5, 1 John 3:17-18). To ignore compassion can open the door to injustice because helping people is the right thing to do. It is something Christians "ought" to do (1 John 3:16).

James, an early church leader and Jesus's brother, agrees saying,

> Come now, you rich, weep and howl for the miseries that are coming upon you. Your riches have rotted and your garments are moth-eaten. Your gold and silver have corroded, and their corrosion will be evidence against you and will eat your flesh like fire. You have laid up treasure in the last days. Behold, the wages of the laborers who mowed your fields, which you kept back by fraud, are crying out against you, and the cries of the harvesters have reached the ears of the Lord of hosts. You have lived on the earth in luxury and self-indulgence. You have fattened your hearts in a day of slaughter. (Jas 5:1–5)

Now, in saying all that, the Bible is also clear that compassion is only for truly needy people. It is never for the reckless, the lazy, the negligent, or the manipulative. Compassion should never enable or encourage these things—doing so would be unjust! We are actually to deprive people like that and refuse to help them so that they get to work. If "anyone is not willing to work, let him not eat" (2 Thess 3:10)! The SJM believes compassion involves things like government welfare, reparations, and not only accepting it with a smile when rioters destroy your city and property, but society should help them do so or its racist, all of which fails to conform to true justice or compassion.

Second, true justice is marked by *retribution*. This is punishment deserved and inflicted for an immoral act. God executes justice based on his perfectly good character and the alignment of a person's actions with his law (Ps 28:4–5, Isa 59:18, Jer 17:10, Ezek 24:14). He always and only gives people exactly what they deserve for their crimes against him (Prov 11:21, 16:5). This is what we mean when we say God is just and we demand people be treated fairly. We want everyone to be treated equally before the law, judged according to what they deserve for their actions. When the guilty are punished and the innocent are safe, that's justice. That is right and good. When the innocent are punished, but the guilty are not, that's injustice (Prov 17:15). God will punish this (Amos 5:11–12, Mal 3:5) because it is wrong and evil (unless, of course, the innocent acts as a substitute for the guilty, being condemned and punished because he willingly takes the crimes of the guilty as if he committed them himself—thank you, Jesus!).

One of the marks of an evil society is injustice (Isa 5:22–23, 10:1–2, 59:14–15; Hab 1:4). There is no justice without the punishment of evil. Romans 13:4 says civil government done right acts as a "servant of God, an avenger who carries out God's wrath on the wrongdoer"—that's retribution! The proof that a government is wicked is those in authority pass laws that promote sin and injustice (Ps 94:20). Justice cannot be done unless and until injustice, sin, and evil have been judged and punished first. This restores peace and harmony to a people where injustice has been given the upper hand (Isa 59:8), and it has a preventing and correcting effect on behavior. Justice means wrongs are actually made right, not compounded by more wrongs committed against more innocent people in the name of social justice. Injustice redefined as justice will only encourage further injustice. This is how social justice advocates bewitch people. Using tools like diversity training, they try to convince men and/or white people particularly that they are guilty of the unforgivable sin of benefiting from systemic oppression. It takes innocent people, who have committed no actual sins against anyone, and brainwashes them into believing they have simply for being white and/or male. Using propaganda and high pressure tactics to convince people that they oppress women or minorities (or have benefitted from it), most are beaten into submission with the ideology and gladly receive punishment from the people they have allegedly oppressed as justice for their imaginary crimes. At the same time, for the so-called oppressed, the goal is for them to adopt a victim mentality that not only holds them back in life, but makes them warriors for the movement who channel their rage at their so-called oppressors when no actual acts of oppression can be identified. In reality, both indoctrination schemes are wicked and unjust.

It is important to note that injustice is also tied to tangible actions (Luke 23:40-41), not feelings or vague pontifications about systems, structures, institutions, and disparities that "everybody knows is unjust" even though no actual laws or policies can be identified as unjust.[1] Injustice needs immoral laws, actual laws being broken that are then going unpunished, or people being punished for breaking laws they did not actually break. Holding someone accountable for things they did not actually do is injustice—plain and simple! Punishing someone for crimes committed by someone else, even in one's own family (Ezek 18:19-20), through activities like looting, rioting, and demanding reparations, is also unjust. It cleverly disguises resentment and greed behind a mask of justice. Being on the side of true justice would guarantee that a person is also for retribution, thus ensuring that he or she will be against any violence perpetrated in the name of social justice.

STUDY QUESTIONS

1. Read Exodus 20:1-20. When you compare your life to God's law, what is the result? What are you going to do about that? What can you do about that?

2. Read 1 John 3:16-18. In what way can you show compassion to someone in your life that truly needs it?

3. Biblically, what is wrong with looting and riots as well as the justifications people give for them?

---

[1] For facts on this, see Thomas Sowell, *Discrimination and Disparities* (New York: Basic Books, 2019).

TRUE JUSTICE VS. SOCIAL JUSTICE, PART 2

Continuing from the previous chapter, the third mark of true justice is *impartiality*. God "judges impartially according to each one's deeds" (1 Pet 1:17). This refers to equal treatment of all people. It's holding everyone to the same standard. It's not a multi-tiered justice system where power, privilege, or the lack thereof means you are treated differently than others for the same actions, which is what social justice activists demand. Impartial justice is what makes judgment fair. This is what Peter means when he says God "judges justly" (1 Pet 2:23). He does not consider who the person is when He judges. He only considers one's action in relation to his law. Injustice includes any hint of favoritism in the application of the law—its penalties or its rewards. This is why justice is portrayed as blindfolded. If Lady Justice has her blindfold up, so that things like wealth, ethnicity, gender, religion, political party, or the results of a decision are taken into account, her verdict will inevitably be unjust.

Deuteronomy 16:18–20a supports this, saying,

You shall appoint judges and officers in all your towns that the LORD your God is giving you, according to your tribes, and they shall judge the people with righteous judgment. You shall not pervert justice. You shall not show partiality, and you shall not accept a bribe, for a bribe blinds the eyes of the wise and subverts the cause of the righteous. Justice, and only justice, you shall follow. (cf. Deut 1:16–17)

Acts 10:34, Romans 2:11, and Galatians 2:6 all give a very simple reason for why we must never enshrine partiality as a virtue in the ways we relate to each other: "God shows no partiality." God is not impressed with ethnicity, gender, money, status, influence, or the lack thereof, and neither should we. Christians are never to prejudge a person or an event before all the facts are in since we are to do nothing from partiality or favoritism (1 Tim 5:21, Jas 2:1). In fact, "if you show partiality, you are committing sin and are convicted by the law as transgressors" (Jas 2:9; cf. Exod 23:3, 6). No one—the poor or the rich, the strong or the weak, the privileged or the underprivileged, the white or the non-white, the oppressor or the oppressed—no one should ever receive preferential treatment from the law. To show anyone special treatment, to look away when they commit crimes, to ignore the law when the law has been broken, is the textbook definition of injustice and unfairness. Wherever this has happened, all over the world, including America, based on things like ethnicity or gender or political party, it is evil, regardless of the justifications for the partiality.

If this happens in the future, in the name of righting past wrongs, for instance, it is equally evil. It is always unjust to give a so-called oppressed group special treatment under the law or to look away from their crimes. This is evil and will never right the wrongs of the past—it merely justifies and perpetuates injustice! "Just and true are [God's] ways" (Rev 15:3). Justice and truth are joined in this text because there is no justice without truth. Leviticus 19:15 says, "You shall do no injustice in court. You shall not be partial to the poor or defer to the great, but in righteousness shall you judge your neighbor." Partiality is never right (Prov 18:5) because it does not conform to God's law. It is wicked to be partial in the application of justice, even if the motive is to fix a real evil that was perpetrated. Two wrongs don't make a right—even kids know this!

We should never seek to address injustice through the application of favoritism. That simply trades one form of injustice for another. Justice is treating the prince and the pauper equally. Where that hasn't happened, partiality is not the answer. It only incites further injustice and injustice addressed though further injustice can never achieve justice. It will only amplify injustice

24

and can lead to anarchy (Prov 22:8). This may be the greatest misunderstanding of justice by the SJM. Ask yourself, is it better for the common good to live under the rule of elites where we know partiality will reign supreme because history tells us that elites will protect their own? Or, is it better for the common good that we uphold and defend the rule of law impartially? The answer is obvious!

Fourth, true justice is *sinless*. God's justice is not always immediate—some ask, "Where is the God of justice?" (Mal 2:17)—but when it comes, his justice is flawless. It is perfect, with no taint of sin, partiality, injustice, error, or unrighteousness whatsoever. God never comes to the wrong conclusion. Nothing He ever does can pervert justice. He is never biased. He has no prejudices. There is not even a hint of self-interest or self-promotion in actual justice. It's not selfish at all, in the sense of manipulating a situation to benefit from it. It is a God who is perfect in goodness that weighs our actions (1 Sam 2:3). He does so by comparing our decisions to his perfect and holy law.

In addition, when justice is sinless, injustice is impossible. Nothing can be missed because "all are naked and exposed to the eyes of [God] to whom we must give account" (Heb 4:13). He "searches all hearts and understands every plan and thought" (1 Chr 28:9) and as a result, "Nothing is covered up that will not be revealed, or hidden that will not be known. Therefore, whatever you have said in the dark shall be heard in the light, and what you have whispered in private rooms shall be proclaimed on the housetops" (Luke 12:2–3).

While God's justice is sinless, spotless, and free from error, sin infects just about everything we do in this life. However, we will inject all manner of error and sin into peoples' lives when we replace justice with social justice. This substitution guarantees injustice. It demands Lady Justice peak from under her blindfold, enshrines favoritism as moral, and replaces facts with feelings, all so that ethnicity, gender, and other categories will cancel God's law (which is expressed in all true laws).

Fifth, justice in the Bible is *inescapable*. For those who look down their noses at sinners, "Do you suppose . . . that you will escape the judgment of God?" (Rom 2:3). That rhetorical question assumes a 'No' answer since God's justice is unavoidable. As just, He will not let even a single transgression go unpunished. He will avenge every sin, right every wrong, address every injustice ever committed by everyone.

I remember being on a walking tour of Berlin in the summer of 2001. As we approached an apartment complex, the guide began telling us about the end of World War II and Hitler's suicide as the Allied Forces closed in on his bunker. At that moment, I was overcome by anger as he talked about Hitler escaping justice near the spot where I was standing. That involuntary anger is an indication that as beings created in God's image, we want justice to be inescapable. We inherently know it is wrong when the guilty get away with their crimes. Justice escaped is injustice. This is why cold case detectives spend decades trying to crack unsolved cases. Deep inside of us, we long for no one to escape justice when a true injustice has taken place. Now, while people like Hitler may be fugitives from justice in this life, justice is inevitable in the next.

Though people may try to hide behind their ethnicity, gender, bank accounts, fame, good deeds, intelligence, or some other kind of privilege, there is not a single person who will be overlooked by God's justice. We can all be "assured [that] an evil person will not go unpunished" (Prov 11:21). There is absolutely no way God will let any violation of his law be rewarded. God will "by no means clear the guilty" (Nah 1:3). There are no protected classes. There are no excuses God will accept. Some people may experience the worst injustices imaginable in this life, but not even that will rescue them from God's justice for their sins. Male and female, white and non-white, educated and uneducated, rich and poor, great and ordinary, known and unknown, moral and immoral—all will be judged according to what they have done (Rev 20:12).

Sixth and finally, the Bible's teachings on true justice will often include *salvation*. Justice is never served in the SJM. There is no hope that a so-called oppressor can ever be free. Their penance, contrition, and restitution must be endless. In contrast,

God offers the only way to be saved from his otherwise inescapable justice. If God demands retribution for every sin we have ever committed, and if his justice is flawless and inescapable, then how can there be any good news at all? When understood rightly, all we should have is "a fearful expectation of judgment" (Heb 10:27). How can there ever be salvation from God's justice? How can there be forgiveness?

On the cross, Jesus did what the SJM cannot do and never even wants to do. He received God's justice for the sins of the world (John 1:29, 3:14-17; 1 John 2:1-2) so that true freedom is offered to all who believe in him (Gal 2:4, 5:1). He became sin on our behalf (2 Cor 5:21) and then took the just, right, and good penalty we sinners deserve (Rom 3:23-26). Justice is just as important to the gospel as the death of Christ. In fact, without justice, there is no death of Christ. The gospel promotes the justice of God just as much as it does his love. If Jesus failed to satisfy God's justice, there is no hope that anyone could ever be saved from it. What makes the gospel good news is that sinners receive mercy because Jesus received our justice.

In the end, social justice is a perversion of true justice! Both paradigms may use the word *justice*, but it is hard to see how they can be any more different in their definitions. So, how did the SJM get into the church? More on that in the next section, but after this chapter, it should be obvious that social justice as a concept was not taken from the Bible. It is not the product of exegesis, which is the study of the text to discover the intention of the author. Sadly, when comparing social justice with God's justice—marked by Compassion, Retribution, Impartiality, Sinlessness, Inescapability, and Salvation—it becomes clear that the SJM creates a CRISIS in regards to true justice. It redefines justice and it fixes nothing! It will not only intensify injustice, but the real crisis is that the SJM's misunderstanding of justice corrupts the gospel. Without true justice, the good news of Jesus's death and resurrection to save sinners from God's wrath is unnecessary, and when sinners are unforgiven, they are not motivated to grant forgiveness (Matt 18:21-35, Luke 7:36-50). This undermining of the gospel makes the SJM a severe evil to stand against, not an analytical tool to integrate with Christianity.

STUDY QUESTIONS

1. Read James 2:1–13. In what ways can a community of people become corrupted by partiality?

2. Read Romans 2:2–11. List as many descriptions as you can of true justice.

3. In your own words, summarize the Bible's teaching on justice.

A COMPLETELY DIFFERENT RELIGION

As the previous chapter demonstrated, the SJM is a "different gospel" (Gal 1:6) because it conflicts with the true gospel in profound ways. It is a new civil religion, a competing worldview, with a distinct theology, philosophy, values, stories, and behaviors. It is not only antithetical to the founding documents of many nations all over the world, like the Declaration of Independence and the United States Constitution, but it is an assault on biblical truth.

For instance, in the SJM, God is replaced by social justice ideology. The system of thought (called neo-Marxism, Cultural Marxism, or Identity Marxism and briefly explained in chapter six) functionally replaces God while setting the tone for the movement, which is something God does for Christians. It is the ultimate authority advocates adhere to without question, not God. If God is considered at all, he is not our Creator-King. Social justice crusaders either use aspects of his character (like his love or his justice) to manipulate God-fearing people or he is relegated to a silent lapdog that is completely subservient to the whims and wishes of the culture.

Also, to social justice adherents the Bible is not truth as Jesus called it (John 17:17). It is merely *a* voice for guidance when it is useful as such. It is not a sufficient authority either (2 Tim 3:16–17). It must be supplemented (and for all practical purposes replaced) by a canon of woke authors whose ideology redefines biblical terms, supersedes biblical theology, and reinterprets the Bible along social justice lines. In the SJM, *truth* is not understood as correspondence to reality and something that applies to all people, in all places, and at all times in history. The idea of truth is pushed as merely individual, societal, or communal even though truth doesn't have a skin color, a gender, or a sexual preference. You can detect this perspective when people talk about "my truth" where they confuse truth with feelings and distinguish truth from facts in the process.

In the SJM, knowledge is not based on revelation, science, evidence, or reason since each of those are considered tools used to oppress people.[1] Instead, *knowledges* are person-specific and based on the "intersections" of oppression a person has. In other words, the more "lived experiences" of oppression a person feels like she has, the more knowledge she has. For instance, based on the teachings of Intersectionality,[2] a woman is more knowledgeable because she is more oppressed than a man. In the intersections of life experience, she will be "hit" by the sexist car for being a woman. A lesbian is more knowledgeable because she is more oppressed than a heterosexual female. She is "hit" by both the sexist and homophobic cars. A black lesbian has more knowledge because she is more oppressed than a white lesbian. A disabled, black lesbian is more knowledgeable because she is more oppressed than an able-bodied, black lesbian. A disabled, black, trans lesbian is more knowledgeable because she is more oppressed than a merely disabled, black lesbian, etc. At the same time, white, heterosexual, Christian males who "identify" as their biological gender have no knowledge to contribute because they are the ultimate oppressors in a world where oppression is considered the ordinary state of affairs. They cannot possibly contribute to identifying or repairing any oppression because they have no "lived experience" of oppression, and therefore, no

---

[1] Andrew Kerr, "Smithsonian Museum Says Objective Thinking Is A Sign of 'Whiteness'," *Daily Caller*, July 15, 2020, accessed July 17, 2020, https://dailycaller.com/2020/07/15/smithsonian-museum-whiteness-objective-thinking/.

[2] This is a view of human interaction that UCLA Law Professor Dr. Kimberlé Crenshaw developed and explained in her groundbreaking article "Mapping the Margins: Intersectionality, Identity Politics, and Violence Against Women of Color," *Stanford Law Review* 46, no. 6 (July 1991). For a critique of this view, see James Lindsay, "Intersectionality,' *New Discourses' Social Justice Encyclopedia*, February 4, 2020, accessed October 29, 2020, https://newdiscourses.com/tftw-intersectionality/.

knowledge of it. If you are from a so-called oppressor class, or you aren't as oppressed as someone else, you are told to just shut up and listen to the oppressed, period!

This conflict between the SJM and the truth doesn't end there. In the SJM, categorizing all people as either oppressors (think white, Christian, heterosexual males who act sexually in line with their biology) or oppressed (everyone else) replaces people being made in our Creator's image. This is essentially an attack on the first page of the Bible! It vilifies teachings like (1) every person of every ethnicity is an image-bearer of God (Gen 1:26–27), (2) there is only one human race (Gen 1:26–30, 2:18–20; Acts 17:26), (3) God made only two genders (Gen 1:27, 5:2; Mark 10:6), (4) God instituted marriage to unite a man and a woman and to start a new family unique from their parents (Gen 2:20–24), and (5) He created men and women as equals in value and dignity (Gen 1:26–27) while giving them complementary responsibilities (leadership for husbands and submission for wives; cf. Gen 2:18, 23)—all this *before* the Fall when sin entered the world! This makes #1-5 above part of God's creation when it was still "very good" (Gen 1:31).

In the SJM, *Original Sin* (the sin all human beings inherited from Adam after the Fall; see Rom 5:12–21) is replaced by white privilege,[3] racism, patriarchy, and/or hetero-normativity (the cultural assumption that heterosexuality is normal). It permanently stains all those in a so-called oppressor class so that no one in that category has the possibility of becoming unstained from it regardless of what they say or do. For instance, if you are considered white, you are stained with white privilege and there is nothing you can do to fix it. If you say you don't have it, that's white fragility.[4] If you say you have it, you're trying to flee your

---

[3] This refers to "the automatic privileges that come with membership in the dominant race" (Richard Delgado and Jean Stefancic, *Critical Race Theory: An Introduction* [New York: New York University Press, 2001], 75).

[4] Developed by Robin DiAngelo in her book *White Fragility*, this refers to the defensive responses, born out of unexamined racial advantage, that white people allegedly have to ideas like systemic racism or white privilege. These

oppression. No one can ever atone for or absolve himself. Being in an oppressor class is similar to the blasphemy of the Spirit (Mark 3:29, Luke 12:10). It renders groups of people unpardonable, unable to be forgiven for their social justice sins.

In the SJM, being born again by God's Spirit (John 3:1–8, Titus 3:5) is exchanged for going woke. This refers to "waking up" to the mass oppression of some groups in a society by other groups in that same society. In the SJM, Jesus and the gospel message that proclaims him as Savior and Lord are replaced by authors who promote the SJM and a false-Jesus who advances their cause.[5] While canceling the true Messiah, like little pseudo-messiahs, they dispense a social justice ideology that "saves" their followers from social justice damnation. They become "saviors" whose work (like Jesus's death and resurrection) gives people the lens through which they should see all of life. This further proves the SJM is an anti-gospel that offers "another Jesus" (2 Cor 11:2–4) with no hope of salvation. Antiracism is antichrist and hides racism behind a façade of fighting racism! Without the slightest chance of forgiveness, the SJM can only offer an endless hamster wheel of confession, penance, and self-flagellation. This is ultimately an attack on the power and proclamation of the cross. Guilt and shame are all you get. If the "oppressed" ever truly forgave their "oppressors," they would not only be letting them off the hook for their oppression, but the whole movement would cease to exist. Forgiveness and salvation are heresy for a movement fueled by demonization and rage.

Justification is God's once-for-all declaration that he forever accepts a sinner when Jesus's righteousness is received by faith in him alone. In the SJM, this is traded for acceptance from cultural elites or the mobs on social media. Nothing broadcasts, "You have my approval" like retweets, likes, and little heart, or

---

responses are then utilized to protect white supremacy, thus perpetuating systemic racism.

[5] Ben Johnson, "'Jesus was a political revolutionary': Ibram X. Kendi 'rejects' orthodox Christianity," *Acton Institute Powerblog*, March 27, 2021, accessed January 23, 2022, https://blog.acton.org/archives/119859-jesus-was-a-political-revolutionary-ibram-x-kendi-rejects-orthodox-christianity.html.

fire, or pointing-finger emojis. This lust for approval creates a never-ending display of one's own righteousness on Facebook, Twitter, Instagram, etc. In the SJM, *sanctification*—growth after salvation into becoming more like Jesus (Rom 8:29)—is transformed into activism, being politically correct, admitting one's guilt as an oppressor, repenting of that oppression, "doing the work" of anti-racism, telling white people they're racists because they're white, considering Black conservatives white supremacists,[6] letting men know they're chauvinists for being men, or damning people in general for being homophobic and/or transphobic. Converting people into social justice warriors, squeezed into the mold of the progressive, socialist political agenda, is the goal. In Christian circles, this false sanctification is seen when doctrinal stands like complementarianism are modified with words like "soft" or "kinder" in the hopes of being relevant to demographic groups that Christians want to appeal to (as if cultural acceptance is *the* key to reaching people for Jesus). It is also seen when Christians repent of biblical doctrines they previously held, but now come across as too conservative politically, or when they rush to a more nuanced and sophisticated "middle road" on something like Critical Race Theory (CRT) by saying things like they are firmly against it while affirming the ideology in the form of things like white privilege, repenting of whiteness, and systemic racism.

In the SJM, *church discipline* is being canceled, which can take the form of being unfriended or blocked on social media, being shunned by friends or family, losing employment, or experiencing physical violence. The irony of this is, social justice advocates will slam groups like the Catholic Church for their inquisition of people like Galileo (who was punished for correctly teaching that the earth revolves around the sun) while they repeat the identical tactic towards all "heresy" against their views.

---

[6] Erika D. Smith, "Larry Elder says he's not a face of white supremacy. His fans make it hard to believe," August 27, 2021, accessed February 18, 2022, https://www.latimes.com/california/story/2021-08-27/larry-elders-recall-fans-prove-hes-face-white-supremacy.

Evangelism becomes working to (1) convince people that they are part of a system of oppression, either as beneficiaries or victims, and (2) to liberate society from this oppression. The actual proclamation of the gospel is no longer about personal salvation from sin, death, and hell.[7] This quickly devolves into virtue signaling, which is letting the world know that you will do your part to stand with the oppressed through empty displays of solidarity that others should admire and emulate while accomplishing next to nothing. *Discipleship* is participating in conversations about alleged oppression with people from so-called oppressed groups. These conversations are meant to enrage people into becoming social justice revolutionaries. Then, as these true believers infiltrate an organization, they will demonize, demoralize, and deconstruct that organization either to transform it into a social justice factory that produces more warriors for their cause or to destroy it from the inside (if there is any significant resistance to the ideology). Many become experts at causing problems and then demanding their solutions be implemented to the problems they caused.

Unity and reconciliation in the SJM are not accomplished through Christ and the gospel. Instead, it comes through shared commitments to dogmas like systemic racism, patriarchy, misogyny, white supremacy, imperialism, white fragility, critical consciousness, diversity, equity, inclusion,[8] colonialism, and the need for social justice. Without total agreement in all of these areas, there is no hope for unity, only an ever-expanding list of so-called "injustices." Finally, *eschatology* (a word used for the Bible's teaching on the end of history) is utopian. Their goal is to overturn all the structures that hold up a society, like the family, media, economy, business, religion, education, government, law, etc., and establish an equitable redistribution of power and

---

[7] Rod Dehrer, "Antichrist, Anti-Christian," *The American Conservative*, March 24, 2021, accessed February 7, 2022. https://www.theamericanconservative.com/dreher/kendi-antiracist-antichristian-critical-race-theory/.

[8] New Discourses, "Understanding Diversity, Equity, and Inclusion," *YouTube*. September 25, 2020, accessed December 22, 2021, https://www.youtube.com/watch?v=Z8XsP5hqK3Y.

resources from the so-called oppressors to those they're said to oppress. If there is any resistance, they will incite a revolution. They will get what they want by any means necessary, without hesitation or mercy.

After comparing the SJM to the biblical worldview, it is obvious that the SJM is a completely different religion—a heartless, godless, Christless, graceless, hopeless cult. It is more than a fad that Christian leaders can ignore, try to use to reach lost people, or help believers grow. It is "a different gospel" because it distorts the gospel, causes people to desert the one, true God, and as such, stands under eternal condemnation (Gal 1:6-8). There cannot be a single good reason why such an obvious heresy like the SJM can have such a massive influence on evangelicalism. Why would any Christian, especially a leader, think that we should embrace this ideology, integrate it into Christianity, and promote it as a better way to live the Christian life? Explanations for resistance against the SJM like white guilt or wanting to be liked make even less sense. Our watchmen have been willing to sacrifice reputation and relationships in the past. They know better than the rest of us that what they are undermining is nothing less than the gospel. It seems they are compromising now for reasons they refuse to be honest about.

This is why, around 2015, when I saw this movement growing in the culture and seeping into the evangelical church, I thought it wouldn't last. "Our watchmen will see this one easily, deal with it decisively, and it'll go away as the other attacks did." I was wrong! Though I should have known better, I was late to this party, but now that I'm here, I hope it is obvious now why every Christian should draw a line in the sand and say to anyone going down this road, "I love you, but against the SJM, I must stand!" As demonstrated above, Christians—and all religious and non-religious people for that matter—now find themselves in a conflict of religions, a second Civil War. This is not a war being fought on battlefields; it's being fought in the realm of ideas through every form of media we have. It's a war of worldviews: the Judeo-Christian worldview of the Bible, which is the basis for what's been normal in the West and other places for centuries, versus the atheistic, man-centered worldview of secularism.

In the face of this confrontation, let J. C. Ryle exhort you from the grave, "When truth is assailed, those who love truth should grasp it more firmly than ever."[9] Oh, I know if you embrace what's said in this book you'll be attacked as a fundamentalist, or worse. Maybe you will be called a racist, sexist, narrow-minded, fragile, uneducated, bigoted, privileged, unloving white supremacist. If this bullying ever happens to you, here's a way to gut the SJM of its influence.[10] It's quite simple. To any attack like these, just say, "I could not care less what you think about me or what you call me. I live for Jesus's approval, not yours." This was Paul's response to the false teachers promoting an anti-gospel heresy in Galatia. He simply asked, "Am I now seeking the approval of man, or of God? Or am I trying to please man? If I were still trying to please man, I would not be a servant of Christ" (Gal 1:10; cf. John 12:42–43, 2 Cor 5:9, 1 Thess 2:4). So, what's it going to be for you? Many Christian leaders are trying to do both, and with tolerant people they can, but not with the SJM. Social justice warriors are warriors; they're anything but tolerant. They are playing an all-or-nothing game that even third way, middle of the road people must eventually submit to. You either bow down or you will be mown down.

Christian, is James 4:4 still in the Bible? Does it still have authority over your life when it says, "You adulterous people! Do you not know that friendship with the world is enmity with God? Therefore, whoever wishes to be a friend of the world makes himself an enemy of God"? Many in the leadership class of evangelicals ignore this verse with slogans like "The world is watching" when it is adulterous to your relationship with God to compromise truth in order to befriend the world. Friendship with the world is a declaration of war on God. So, have we now become

---

[9] J. C. Ryle, *Knots Untied: Being Plain Statements on Disputed Points in Religion* (London: William Hunt and Company, 1885), 110.

[10] For a myriad of theological and philosophical responses to the SJM, see the Recommended Resources in appendix 1.

smarter than the Bible? Can we befriend the world in the hopes of reaching the world for the God we declare war on when we befriend the world? One of my pastors used to say to us, "You can be faithful or popular, but you can only pick one." In the case of the SJM, this statement could not be truer.

Instead, we must "stand firm" in the "true grace of God" (1 Pet 5:12) when divine truth is being molested. We must stand with Christ and his faithful followers down through the ages. We must stand against the world, especially when the world, with its anti-God philosophies, infiltrates the church (2 Cor 10:5). We must not bow; we must not kneel (Dan 3:18). We must stand because we love the truth. We must stand because we love the gospel. We must stand because we love our neighbors, even the ones who attack us for not joining them in their social justice revolution. We must stand because we believe there is still hope that like many other unbiblical movements that tried to sabotage the church, this one will be exposed, confronted, and removed as well.

So, how did we get here? How did this "Trojan horse"[11] make its way into the evangelical church, disguised as a friend while waiting for the perfect time to attack us from the inside? Great question, which we will explore in Part 2.

STUDY QUESTIONS

1. Explain the social justice view of truth and knowledge in contrast to the biblical view of truth and knowledge.

---

[11] Sovereign Nations, "The Trojan Horse," *YouTube*, August 9, 2019, accessed November 5, 2019, https://www.youtube.com/watch?v=YDFL3xwEEG8. No Christian has been fighting against today's SJM longer and at a greater personal cost than Michael O'Fallon. We owe him a debt of gratitude for sounding the alarm well before most of us had any clue how much danger we were actually in.

2. Explain the social justice view of humanity in contrast to the biblical view of humanity.

3. Explain the social justice view of Jesus and the gospel in contrast to the biblical view of Jesus and the gospel.

PART 2

WHAT IF CHRISTIANS DON'T STAND AGAINST THE SOCIAL JUSTICE MOVEMENT?

A DARKER REMAKE OF THE FAILED ORIGINAL

Several similarities between Paul's letter to the Galatian churches and today's Social Justice Movement (SJM) make it a template for understanding what's going on today (Parts 1 and 2) and how Christians should respond to it (Part 3). Like the Galatian heresy, the SJM is covertly injecting a theological poison into the Body of Christ. It is the worst kind of poison, the kind that trusted people promote as perfectly safe, able to fix a problem and make us healthy, all while feeling good as it goes in. In reality, it enters the host, attacks, weakens, and kills off parts of the body.

The problems we are being told evangelicals foment—but that the SJM claims to fix—are issues like racism, sexism, disparities, and homophobia. However, the solutions social justice advocates push for are far from biblical principles. Their solution is the redistribution of things like influence, affluence, opportunities, and privileges from so-called advantaged groups to so-called disadvantaged groups. R.C. Sproul once said he could not think of many other concepts that are more misleading in our contemporary culture than social justice. That's because while justice has to do with the rule of law and righteousness in a culture, social justice, he said rightly, is a synonym for *socialism*.[1] This is an economic theory marked by government ownership of industry and total control over the supply of goods to the population. Governments that sought to implement this in the

---

[1] R. C. Sproul, "R.C. Sproul on Social Justice," *YouTube*, June 5, 2011, accessed November 5, 2020, https://www.youtube.com/watch?v=LI-yiwrVhhn0&t=375. For helpful insights into socialism, also see PragerU, "Why Socialism Never Works: A Video Marathon," *YouTube*, December 30, 2021, accessed January 5, 2022, https://www.youtube.com/watch?v=v_eobnhtCy8.

twentieth century (e.g., Russia, China, Korea, Cambodia, Cuba, Vietnam, etc.) are responsible for around 100 million deaths.

Today's SJM is not just advocating for the economics of classic socialism. It demands equity, meaning proponents see no justice until everyone in a society is equal, not in income, but in outcomes and privileges. Any disparity beyond certain (often arbitrary) thresholds between groups is used as evidence of racism, sexism, oppression, etc.[2] This is the economic theory of Marxism integrated with disciplines like sociology and psychology, which is why it is often called neo-Marxism.[3] Mix neo-Marxism with postmodern philosophy, as well as racial, feminist, and queer studies, and you have the majority of today's SJM.

They demand that *groups* of people be held accountable or receive rewards simply because everyone in a group is automatically guilty or innocent depending solely on which group a person belongs to. For example, white people are automatically guilty of racism. Men are automatically guilty of sexism. Heterosexuals are automatically homophobic and transphobic, simply because of the group they belong to, not because of anything they actually do. They are oppressors because they benefit from the alleged cultural power of their group and use that power, often without knowing it, to oppress people of color, women, and the LGBT community.

The redistribution of power, wealth, opportunities, and privileges from advantaged groups to disadvantaged groups is likely not the goal of every Christian who is sympathetic to the SJM. They want to honor God and do something loving about what they perceive to be racism, sexism, etc. and think the pathway to doing so is social justice. However, redistribution is the mission of the SJM overall. Its teachings slither past our watchmen and into pulpits where it seduces unsuspecting victims whose defenses are down—after all, they're at church!—as social justice is

---

[2] James Lindsay, "Equity," *New Discourses*, July 13, 2020, accessed December 21, 2021, https://newdiscourses.com/tftw-equity.

[3] James Lindsay, "Neo-Marxism," *New Discourses*, May 31, 2021, accessed December 22, 2021, https://newdiscourses.com/tftw-neo-marxism.

stealthily and illegitimately inserted into biblical texts on justice. This is done through modifying the definitions of ancient Greek and Hebrew words and themes with twenty-first century, neo-Marxist definitions. This bewitches people into thinking social justice directives are biblical (Gal 3:1, 5:8). Then, these directives are pushed as God's will to punish or reward people for things they did or didn't do. This institutionalizes partiality in the name of a God who shows no partiality (Eph 6:9). The command to love your neighbor (Matt 22:39) becomes supporting the Black Lives Matter organization, radical feminism, homosexual marriage, gender reassignment in children, and trans athletes. Keeping in step with the gospel (Gal 2:14) becomes admitting white guilt and white fragility, confessing misogyny, lamenting white privilege, doing the work of anti-racism, and repenting of hetero-normativity. This dresses the wolf of injustice in the sheep's clothing of biblical justice, deceiving Christians into thinking evil is good when the SJM remains a truth-distorting evil.

This gospel-twisting redefinition of justice is nothing new. The same thing happened over a hundred years ago. Most of you reading this likely identify yourself as a Protestant evangelical. Evangelicalism, as we know it today, is the result of a controversy that split much of Protestantism between modernists and fundamentalists. Back then, a fundamentalist was someone who believed in and defended the core teachings of Christianity. These are the Inspiration of the Bible (that the Bible came from God as the primary source), Jesus's Virgin Birth, the reality of his miracles, his death as a substitute for sinners, the historical reliability of his resurrection, and his Second Coming.

You might think, "If you reject those things, you're not a Christian," and you would be right! However, those who denied these essential Christian doctrines, the modernists, continued to call themselves Christians because they held on to a kind of Christian ethic. For them, the core of Christianity was moral, not theological—"Deeds not creeds," they cried. Like today, Christian words were redefined along politically progressive lines. Back then, it wasn't called the SJM; it was called the Social

Gospel, Social Christianity, or Christian Socialism because it replaced the gospel of individual salvation from sin, death, and hell with corporate salvation from societal and economic deprivation. What they taught resembled Karl Marx more than Jesus Christ while at the same time claiming they were more faithful followers of Jesus than the fundamentalists.

The social order, they said, is sinful and it corrupts all the individuals that live in it. Faith in Jesus may save people from their sins, but the effect of structural sin must still be uprooted. Therefore, true Christians should fight societal problems. To fail to do so, they said, was to deny the gospel and could be proof that one's claim to salvation is false. Moreover, structural sin was addressed through the Social Gospel's call to corporate repentance for collective expressions of sin and oppression. This led to advocating for child labor laws, improving working conditions, fixing labor disputes, overhauling economic structures, education reform, a living wage, a fair workweek, improving urban living standards, the prohibition of alcohol, the "christianization" of politics, women's right to vote, and world peace.

Now, are some of those good things to support? Of course! Can supporting some of these things be an outgrowth of the gospel? Sure! Is advocating these things the primary mission of the church? Absolutely not! The mission of the church is worshipping God because of the gospel (1 Cor 10:31), equipping the saints in the gospel (Eph 4:11–13), and reaching the lost with the gospel (Matt 28:18–20). As a part of this, the church should not be uncaring towards the plight of those in need. We are expected to be zealous for good works and to meet legitimate needs (Rom 15:25–27, Titus 3:14, 1 John 3:17–18). However, the danger then and now is confusing this with the church's mission.

The result of the Social Gospel was the splitting of denominations, seminaries, colleges, and churches, and leaving behind the apostate mainline denominations in its wake. These churches continue to meet all over the world, especially in the eastern United States and Europe, typically in massive buildings with very tiny congregations. They are parrots of progressive political platforms rather than the Scriptures. They have no power and very little influence because they turned their back on the core of the Christian message. Without the gospel, there is no mission. Once people compromise on the fundamental doctrines of biblical Christianity, while still trying to be identified as a Christian, the SJM becomes their natural home.

Evangelicalism came out of a split within fundamentalism around the 1950s, led primarily by the magazine *Christianity Today* and the evangelist Billy Graham. After seventy or so years, what we have in evangelicalism today is a multi-decade attack on the Bible from "evangelical" scholars who lust after respectability from unbelievers.[4] Some baptize their thirst for acceptance and influence with non-Christians by calling it evangelism. This has led some leaders to reject Christianity altogether while others try to hold on to their Christian roots by joining a movement called Progressive Christianity, which is just another name for apostasy. Other leaders, the truly despicable ones, stay within evangelical circles and get paychecks from institutions they are knowingly subverting the doctrinal standards of with their influence.

These are the worst kinds of leaders. They are wolves in shepherd's clothing, who sign doctrinal statements they don't believe in, redefine words to mean something they know the statement doesn't mean by those terms, and play shell games like "We only teach *about* Critical Race Theory and Intersectionality" when they advance CRT/I or hire other people to advance it. They are cowards who, in disobedience to the God who knows their hearts (Ps 44:21, John 2:23–25), flirt with, integrate, or fully embrace anti-biblical theories and treat them as helpful to sound doctrine when Christians are told to reject these kinds of ideologies outright (Ps 1:1, Col 2:8, 1 Tim 4:1–2). If leaders like this do not come to their senses and repent (like Peter and Barnabas did in Galatia) their "condemnation from long ago is not idle, and their destruction is not asleep" (2 Pet 2:3; cf. 2 Cor 11:13–15, Gal 1:6-9).

---

[4] Apologia Acts 17:17, "Francis Schaeffer—The Watershed of the evangelical World," *YouTube*, March 12, 2012, accessed February 13, 2022, https://www.youtube.com/watch?v=cXvzvivdVlA.

Because of their lies, subversion, and promotion of error these "leaders" should be exposed publicly and fired immediately (1 Tim 5:20–21). They should never be allowed to return to places of prominence within evangelicalism without public confession and a repentance that is proved over time by their deeds (Acts 26:20, 2 Cor 7:9-11). Partiality and a lack of courage at this point is how the SJM imbeds itself in the church. To be respected, relevant, influential, accepted, and admired, many evangelicals are embracing some form of the SJM, which is merely the latest in a long line of attacks on God's truth. However, today's SJM is a much darker remake of the failed Social Gospel original. This is because the potential for damage is exceedingly worse. While denying the gospel and splitting churches, modernists within the Social Gospel Movement never justified the hatred and violence we see spewing out of the SJM today. This behavior is antithetical to Christianity, but it's normal for gospel-assaulting factions saturated with Marxism.

In Galatians, like in the SJM, we see that when the gospel is attacked, not only does it lose its saving power, but it also damages the lives Christians live. This is what happened to Peter. Galatians 2:11–14 says that when Peter first arrived in Antioch, he had no problem going to a church where both Jews and non-Jews (referred to as "Greeks" or "Gentiles" in the New Testament) worshipped Jesus together. He had become very influential since he was with Jesus daily for 2-3 years and was one of his first followers (John 1:35–42). This alone would make him a hero, not to mention his obvious leadership on the day of Pentecost and beyond. Additionally, he not only associated with Gentiles in Antioch, but he lived "like a Gentile" (2:14). He had no fear of eating foods or disregarding customs that separated Jews from Gentiles or being "contaminated" by relationships with Gentile believers. His actions were a model of the gospel for all Christians to follow.

Sadly, a group of Jews[5] came to Antioch and made Peter uncomfortable with being so close to Gentiles. Maybe they

---

[5] They are known as Judaizers because they "judaized" the gospel by adding OT laws to faith in Jesus for salvation.

confronted him about it. Maybe their looks and demeanor imposed their disapproval on him. Whatever it was, Peter changed his practice out of fear (2:12). To please one man or group of people, he chose to mistreat a second group of people in the church. This is not the first time Peter lacked courage in the face of opposition (Mark 14:66–72), but because he had become so influential, other Jewish Christians in Antioch followed his example (even Barnabas!) and started separating themselves from Gentile Christians too.

This was not just a slight alteration in behavior. This was a radical shift. Peter's actions screamed that believing in Jesus was not enough for God's acceptance because it was not enough for his acceptance. A non-Jewish person must believe in Jesus *and* become Jewish for the great Peter to spend time with him. He fell under the influence of this group of "false brothers" (2:4) though he did not become a false teacher himself. He did not reject the gospel like this group Paul calls "the circumcision party" (2:12) — which sounds like the worst party ever! However, because he allowed this group to influence him, his sanctification suffered, as did his credibility. His actions were out of step with the gospel (2:14). At best, his actions told the Gentile Christians there were two "Bodies" of Christ, a Jewish one and a non-Jewish one, and these two groups were not equal with God. Jewish Christians were far superior to the Gentiles. At worst, his actions told the Gentile Christians they weren't saved at all.

Paul saw the implications of this sinful hypocrisy as an attack on the gospel, so he went to war (2:11)! With incredible courage, he openly confronted the great Peter to his face, not behind his back. He did it publicly (2:14) because Peter's sin was public. If Paul was too intimidated to do this, the Gentile Christians would have thought faith alone is not enough to be accepted by God. It must instead be faith plus the works of the law to be right with God because only then will Peter interact with them again. This would have split the early church into one church for the Jews and another church for non-Jews. Paul could not stand by while this was happening.

The parallels with the SJM are astonishing, not just in the distortion of the gospel (Part 1), but how that distortion plays itself out in the lives of those who fall under its spell. First, high-profile Christian leaders with a lot of exposure to the truth propagate a radical deception. Second, other leaders courageously stand in opposition to all who are attacking the gospel whether they were aware of doing so (like the false teachers in Galatia) or unaware of doing so (like Peter and Barnabas). Third, an attack on the gospel could lead to the severing of relationships among Christians and the splitting of churches. Fourth, faith alone in Jesus must be supplemented, this time by doing the work of social justice. Finally, if left unaddressed, the result will be two competing "Christianities" instead of a single, united body from every tribe, language, people group, and nation—on earth as it will be in heaven (Rev 5:9-10). All of this sounds strikingly similar to the poisonous results of both the Social Gospel Movement of the twentieth century and the SJM that's spreading throughout evangelicalism today, doesn't it?

STUDY QUESTIONS

1. Romans 15:25–27 and 1 John 3:17–18. Is it possible to live out these verses and avoid becoming a social justice warrior? Please explain.

2. After making it this far into *Stand*, how is the SJM out of "step with the truth of the gospel" (Gal 2:14)?

3. As you consider Galatians 2:11–14, what steps did Paul take to identify the problems with Peter's actions and address the false teaching? How does what Paul did with Peter give you insight into how best to respond to the SJM?

FOUR TRUTHS THAT FIGHT DISUNITY

For social justice philosophy to take hold among a group of Christ's followers, as the false teaching did in Galatia, specific truths must be downplayed, obscured, or even denied. In the place of these doctrines, an error must be substituted to muddy the waters and make the error sound true. If this does not happen, if the truth stands firm, Christ's people are inoculated from the lies being injected into it. Protection from the strife and disunity caused both by the Galatian heresy, and by today's SJM, come from at least four permanent realities every Christian enjoys regardless of ethnicity or gender.

The first is *adoption*. Speaking to a church divided into Jews and Gentiles, Paul stated this truth to supersede all barriers, "in Christ Jesus you are *all* sons of God, through faith" (Gal 3:26; emphasis mine). One of the reasons Jesus came to earth was "so that we might receive adoption as sons" (Gal 4:5;m cf. Rom 8:15). Every disciple of Jesus goes from being a criminal condemned before God's law to a son forever received by God's grace. The SJM is committed to dividing us based on arbitrary categories, but God is the Father of every Christian and we are all related to one another as his sons.[1] It attacks the heart of our unity to argue that social justice ideologies are truer and more defining than what Christians are now and forever will be, which is adopted.

The second permanent benefit every Christian has is *union with Christ*. To a church where what's distinctive about different groups was being highlighted as all-important, Paul reminded

---

[1] As an aside, both male and female Christians are considered sons of God because in the ancient world the sons received the inheritance. If you're a woman reading this and its weird to think of yourself as a son of God, imagine being a man who has to see himself as the Bride of Christ!

them "as many of you as were baptized into Christ have put on Christ" (Gal 3:27). This refers to spiritual baptism, which is the invisible but very real immersing of every believer "in Christ," a reality spoken of over a hundred times in the New Testament. Like putting on clothes, we all metaphorically put on Christ, so that we are in him as he completely envelops us spiritually. The SJM demands that our ethnicity, skin color, gender, bank account, or sexual preference unite us with some people while dividing us from others. However, the Bible is clear that every Christian is surrounded by Jesus's love, his life, his presence, and his sinless perfection, and therefore, we are indestructibly united to one another in him.

The third benefit all Christians permanently enjoy is *family*. God could not be any clearer on this, calling Christians adopted (Rom 8:15) and asserting that "There is neither Jew nor Greek, there is neither slave nor free, there is no male and female, for you are *all* one in Christ Jesus" (Gal 3:28; emphasis mine). If God is your Father by faith in Christ (John 1:12), then every Christian is your family member (Eph 3:15). He makes all of us one. We must stop fighting against each other and refuse to see ourselves as separate from each other because in Jesus we are one (John 17:20–23, Rom 12:10). This means ethnicity and gender should never make anyone a second-class citizen in the church, with one ethnicity or one gender treated as superior to another. This is what happened in Galatia, with the Jewish Christians looking down on the Gentile Christians and forcing them to believe in Jesus and become Jewish in order to be accepted.

First, the distinction "Jew and Greek" (3:28) is not racial. In fact, a case can be made that there is no such thing as the modern concept of race in the Bible anyway. The people who invented the idea were opposed to the Bible's ethical teachings as well as its anthropology,[2] which is that we all have the same parents, Adam and Eve (Gen 1:26–28). We all have the same human nature. We are all created in the image of God and all of us can come together

---

[2] James Lindsay, "Race," *New Discourses*, February 5, 2020, accessed January 17, 2022, https://newdiscourses.com/tftw-race/.

with the opposite gender to make more humans. While differences exist between ethnicities on the level of biology and genetics, they turn out to be statistically irrelevant. I should know. According to my DNA profile, I am a mixture of over a dozen European, Russian, Baltic, Polynesian, and Japanese ethnicities. My ancestors got around—without ethnic hatred, I might add—and they could do so because there is only one human race (Acts 17:26).

Now, there are certainly ethnicities with physical features, history, and customs that are similar between people within different ethnic groups. These features are not moral, meaning ethnic groups with certain features are no better or worse than others. It is hardly justifiable to promote racism based on such wonderful characteristics when we can actually learn from, come to enjoy, and have our lives enriched by our differences. In addition, similarities within a group do not necessarily describe every person in a given group. In other words, common features, history, and customs within one ethnicity or nationality do not determine everything about everyone within that ethnicity. People can be different compared to others within their same group. There is no monolithic ethnic culture, like an African-American culture or a white culture, because each person and each experience is unique. The concept of race has been used to overemphasize our differences in order to make them essential to each group, which forces us to stay divided, makes us antagonistic, and allows people with real ethnic hatred to justify horrific atrocities.

Next, the distinction "Jew and Greek" (3:28) is actually a covenantal distinction, in that God made the promises of salvation to the Jews only (Rom 9:1–5, Eph 2:11–12). Reading race into this phrase takes it out of context by inserting a concept into it that would not have occurred to the original author or audience. But think about it, even if this phrase had a basis in ethnic differences, Paul used only one term to describe all non-Jewish ethnicities, "Greek" (cf. Rom 1:16, 3:9, 10:12; 1 Cor 12:13, Col 3:11). By lumping all non-Jews together with one term, it shows that all non-Jewish ethnicities are already united. Russians and Chinese,

Africans and Europeans, Indians and Germans, and even differ-ent kinds of Americans are all "Greeks" or "Gentiles" compared to Jews. We are united, not in our ethnicities, but in our aliena-tion from God's work in the OT. We are united in our need for a Savior, our need to benefit from God's promises, and our hope-less state apart from him (Eph 2:12). However, by God's grace, all Christians are also united in our experience of adoption and un-ion with Christ because each one of us is a member of the same family.

In Galatians 3:28 we learn "there is neither slave nor free." These are not racial categories either. These are social, economic, and class categories, all of which disappear as significant for sal-vation at the foot of the cross and should therefore have no bear-ing on our interaction. Lastly, "there is no male or female," meaning in salvation neither gender has more or less advantage than the other. Women and men are equally saved in Christ who did away with the gender barriers that separated men and women in Judaism, the covenantal barriers that separate Jews and non-Jews, and the social barriers that separate slaves and free people. We are all united in Christ, equal in God's favor, equal in God's acceptance, equal in God's love all because of Je-sus's death and resurrection while still maintaining our God-de-signed differences.

The final permanent benefit every Christian has is an *inher-itance*. This severely divided congregation was counseled with

> If you are Christ's, then you are Abraham's offspring, heirs according to promise. . . . God sent forth his Son, born of woman, born under the law, to redeem those who were un-der the law, so that we might receive adoption as sons. And because you are sons, God has sent the Spirit of his Son into our hearts, crying, "Abba! Father!" So, you are no longer a slave, but a son, and if a son, then an heir through God. (Gal 3:29, 4:4-7; cf. Rom 8:14-17, Titus 3:7)

All that Jesus has from God—all the love, all the blessings, all the acceptance, all the benefits—belongs to people forever when they believe. It is not that his benefits are given to some but not others. Acceptance with God is an eternal reality for all Christians because God fully accepts the Christ we are all in. The love of God is all of ours today because God loves Jesus, and since his love for Jesus is infinite, his love for us is infinite too (see John 17:23, a verse I look at frequently just to make sure it's still there!). In Christ, sinless perfection belongs to every one of us today because Jesus is righteous. He is holy from all eternity and He only ever did what is right according to God's Word during his earthly life. We have all of that because of Jesus, not because we earned our way into the family with good works, not because we keep ourselves in the family by good works (Gal 3:1-3), and not because we are part of a group that the SJM has arbitrarily said is more or less privileged than others.

In the end, the SJM rebuilds walls between people and seeks to create new ones between Christians. These are barriers that Jesus tore down when He died and rose again (Eph 2:11-18). The SJM infects churches like a virus so that we quarantine ourselves from people we will be in heaven with forever. It attacks the four realities we all enjoy as Christians, which weakens the spiritual glue that unites us in the structure he is building. That structure is the church, a new temple, founded on Jesus and the NT authors, where God himself is pleased to dwell (Eph 2:19-22). This is why faithful Christians do well to stand against it vehemently when the SJM invades their lives. The Bible, the gospel, the work of Christ on the cross, the apostles' teaching, and church history all stand against the SJM. Will you?

STUDY QUESTIONS

1. Read Galatians 3:26-29. List all of the ways every Christian is united to every other Christian because they are all trusting in Jesus.

2. Read Galatians 4:1–7. List all of the ways every Christian is united to every other Christian because they are all trusting in Jesus.

3. In what ways do the unifying truths you discovered in Galatians 3:26–4:7 contradict the SJM and its ability to divide Christians from each other.

AN OXYMORONIC CONTRADICTION

Based on what we have seen so far, is social justice ideology taught anywhere in Galatians, a letter written to help address a divided New Testament church? If a NT letter was going to have content that matches social justice ideology, it would be Galatians. However, is there any focus on the need for Christians to repent of their ethnicity and topple the so-called systemic injustice in their society? Does the text show the need for one group of Christians to understand themselves as oppressed by other Christians or institutions? Is there even one legitimate distinction between ethnicities based on the gospel? Are specific ethnicities to be seen as more privileged in society than others? Is the redistribution of power, resources, and privilege from oppressors to the oppressed advocated for in Galatians? Were the Jews told they needed to share their privilege or have them forcibly taken away from them through a cultural revolution and given to the oppressed Gentiles who didn't receive God's promises as they had? Were the Gentiles chastised for the wicked ways other Gentiles treated the Jews in the past? Are Christians to recognize that because of their ethnicity, gender, or sexuality that they're guilty of oppression, of sins only they can commit without even knowing it? Are people racist simply because of the lack of melanin shading their skin, sexist based exclusively on what gender they are, homophobic for supporting biblical marriage, or transphobic because they have the audacity to raise their kids based on the biology God created them to have in the womb?

The answer to all of those questions is a resounding NO! The SJM doesn't get its ideology from the Bible. Their solutions don't come from exegeting biblical texts in the original languages to determine the author's intent in what he wrote. It is nowhere found in the apostles' teachings that were "once for all delivered to the saints" (Jude 3). Social justice ideology is added to the Bible (Rev 22:18) in an attempt to mystify its meaning and manipulate God's people. For social justice advocates, the Bible is insufficient. They insert modern, man-made philosophies into the Bible (Col 2:8), twisting inspired texts to say what they never meant, all to convince people it's loving to catch a ride on the hateful and heretical social justice train. I use the word "heretical" on purpose. As Part 1 demonstrated, the SJM is a different religion, a cult, an anti-gospel, not a secondary issue Christians should disagree about agreeably.

To make a case for the SJM, adherents must downplay, obscure, and/or condemn the permanent realities of adoption, union, family, and inheritance that Jesus gives all who believe in him. They knowingly or unknowingly deny the gospel and the unifying fruit of the gospel, both of which have been preached to audiences made up of different ethnicities, histories, social statuses, economic classes, and genders for 2000 years. Just because batches of Christians have not lived these realities with strict consistency does not mean it fails to be true. Christianity may very well be the first and is certainly the most influential transnational, trans-ethnic, trans-social movement in history! Jesus, the Savior and Lord of all (Luke 2:11), destroys every barrier between us that sin has caused and encourages. All over the world, Christianity has actually done and continues to do what the SJM only believes it can do, but has miserably failed at thus far.

All the talk these days of reconciliation among Christians is meaningless without recognizing that Jesus already accomplished the work and He did it in our place when He reconciled us to God and to each other through his death (Eph 2:11-19). We cannot let social justice ideology create rage in our souls and conflict in our relationships. We must live in the unity Jesus achieved and protect it vigorously in our relationships (Eph 4:3-6), knowing the work to unite us has already been done, and it was done *for* us, not by us. We receive the reconciliation Jesus achieved. We get peace with God *and* every Christian, and we get it from Jesus and at his expense. We are all united in Christ—one Lord, one faith, one baptism—so we should make every effort to keep the unity that the Spirit creates and Jesus achieved. The "bond of peace" (Eph 4:3) that unites Christians must be strongly defended among us regardless of our differences.

This, however, is utterly impossible while adopting social justice ideologies that destroy peace by inciting hatred and division. The prescription the NT gives for dealing with social justice advocates in the church, because they cause division based on false doctrine, is to avoid them and excommunicate them (Rom 16:17-20, Titus 3:10-11). They are the divisive ones, not those who seek to defend the truth and protect God's people from their deception. How many of us would have the courage to carry that out though? It is good, right, and virtuous to avoid and expose false teaching as well as exposing racism, sexism, classism, and every other sinful form of hatred for people Jesus died for. If you are a part of promoting any of that, you should repent, even if you're doing it in the name of social justice. Using the tools of social justice to battle racism or sexism, however, is like fighting a ninja with a hot dog—failure is inevitable!

However, just know this, the social justice goal is not the end of oppression. Oppression is a wedge used to insert socialism into a group, making the SJM a threat not only to the gospel, but also to justice and basic human rights. That statement is not meant to be hyperbolic or inflammatory. Social justice ideology has been a threat to justice in history and it continues to be a threat throughout our world to this very day. Tens of millions of people have been murdered, many of them with government sanction, in the name of social justice. Read the histories of Russia, China, and Cuba, just in the twentieth century (some have been provided in appendix 1), to see what social justice does to real people.[1]

The SJM is also a threat to the gospel because it substitutes God's free grace in Jesus alone for a never-ending hamster wheel

---

[1] See Jonathan Glover, *Humanity: A Moral History of the Twentieth Century* (New Haven, CT: Yale University Press, 2001).

STAND: CHRISTIANITY VS. SOCIAL JUSTICE

of confessing (mostly imaginary) sins, acts of penance, and permanent self-hate with absolutely no hope of forgiveness. The attention and applause one gets from virtue signaling that you're a racist may feel good for a time, but how long can someone do that without the cleansing that forgiveness brings? For social justice adherents, forgiveness is an utterly rejected behavior. To forgive anyone in an oppressor class is to surrender to the oppressor, letting him off the hook for his oppression when no oppressor should ever be allowed to do enough work to clear themselves fully of their "crimes." It doesn't take a rocket scientist to see that the tools of social justice can never do what "the sword of the Spirit, which is the Word of God" (Eph 6:17) has done and continues to do to decimate error and unite people the world over.

For instance, some social justice proponents argue the most threatening racist movement today is not the white supremacy of groups like the KKK. It is the regular American's desire for a race-neutral, color-blind society, which many of us accepted as right from Dr. Martin Luther King's "I Have a Dream" speech. Every day, white men and women are the greatest propagators of racism and bigotry because they dare to think about people *without* regard to their ethnicity, something social justice advocates condemn as racist.[2] Some even say places like America, which had slavery, are more racist now than when it was legal to buy and sell other human beings. This is because racism is now hidden and accepted as normal without the vast majority of people even knowing it.[3] This and much more makes today's SJM far from an extension of the Civil Rights Movement. They use it to position themselves favorably in the larger culture while distinguishing themselves from it in their writings[4] and endorsing

---

[2] For an example of this, see Ibrim X. Kendi, *How to Be an Antiracist* (New York: One World, 2019), 20.

[3] If that sounds like a conspiracy theory, that's because it is. See Robin DiAngelo, *White Fragility: Why It's So Hard for White People to Talk About Racism* (Boston: Beacon Press, 2018), 50.

[4] See Delgado and Stefancic, 2–3, 87, 101 where they admit to challenging the Civil Rights Movement and wanting to change its paradigm.

ideas that if entrenched in our laws would undermine and even violate the Civil Rights Act of 1964.

This insanity, this expression of the depraved, futile, corrupt, darkened mind and hardened heart (Rom 1:28, Eph 4:17–18, Col 1:21, 2 Tim 3:8), is the same poisonous well that unbiblical, illogical, unsubstantiated, and racist concepts emerge from like structural, institutional, or systemic racism, patriarchy, repenting of whiteness, toxic masculinity, white fragility, unconscious bias, or white supremacy attached to white people simply for being white. Whenever you hear these things, no matter who you hear them from, even if it comes from trusted pastors, professors, and authors, just know they are using social justice categories to make their point, even if they say they reject the SJM and CRT/I. Leaders will say this privately and fearfully refuse to take a public stand against the SJM while happily taking stands against, mocking, and even expressing disdain for brothers and sisters who are defending the truth and simply want them to lead from the Bible with clarity, conviction, and courage on these issues. It seems that for far too many Christian leaders their only conviction is not having any convictions (except that they're not a "right winger" or a "fundamentalist") while disparaging and minimizing those that do as extremists who lack the capacity for things like nuance and being winsome.

The SJM and the philosophies that inspired it are not antiracist. Its proponents do not fight racism, sexism, classism, or all the phobias. They promote and perpetuate them by arousing hatred in so-called oppressed groups for so-called oppressor groups, and justify it as moral. Interestingly, they say almost nothing about oppression in countries outside the U.S. That's because if there was a magic wand that removed ethnic or gender discrimination from our world today the leaders of the SJM would oppose it. Ending racism or sexism works against their best interests. Without the boogeyman of oppression always haunting our lives, they become irrelevant (and poor!). Therefore, they have a vested, personal, and even financial interest in constantly re-erecting and fortifying barriers between us that the Judeo-

Christian worldview, Jesus's work on the cross, and the message of the gospel tore down once and for all.

The SJM is an oxymoronic contradiction. It is not social (except as we saw earlier where R. C. Sproul said the "social" in social justice is short for socialism). It is anti-social because it divides people from each other and makes it impossible to bring us together unless social justice ideology is fully embraced on their terms. Second, it does not promote justice. It redefines justice to obscure true justice while promoting and institutionalizing injustice. Along those lines, it can't celebrate diversity or tolerance. Instead, it is a freedom-sabotaging tyranny that destroys both diversity and tolerance since the only acceptable views are those approved by the SJM. That's why black, female, and gay conservatives are so viciously attacked—"not all skin-folk are kinfolk," as the saying goes. They are not even considered diverse because diversity in the SJM means a person of color who must also advocate for social justice ideology. Anything less than complete allegiance is heresy against the SJM and must be canceled. This intolerance has the potential to be at least as bad or, God-forbid, even worse than any religious inquisition in the Middle Ages. Without God and his Word constraining behavior, social justice promoters see themselves as morally superior to all social justice nonconformists and the ends always justify the means, regardless of how unethical the means might be. This is why we saw very little condemnation of the billions of dollars of destruction and violence from mainstream outlets in the summer of 2020. Some excused or minimized it while others blatantly encouraged it.[5]

---

[5] Tristan Justice, "28 Times Media And Democrats Excused Or Endorsed Violence Committed By Left-Wing Activists," *The Federalist*, January 7, 2021, accessed January 26, 2022, https://thefederalist.com/2021/01/07/28-times-media-and-democrats-excused-or-endorsed-violence-committed-by-left-wing-activists; Andrew Kerr, "Here are 31 Times the Media Justified or Explained Away Rioting and Looting After George Floyd's Death," *The Daily Signal*, September 4, 2020, accessed January 27, 2022, https://www.dailysignal.com/2020/09/04/here-are-31-times-the-media-justified-or-explained-away-rioting-and-looting-after-george-floyds-death/.

Make no mistake, resistance, dialogue, or just asking questions, not to mention agreeing to disagree—you know, actual tolerance!—is all bigotry in the SJM. This dogma is an acid that erodes unity in everything it touches unless you shut up, listen, repent, and bow down to the tyranny. It is sinfully judgmental. They have an almost magical ability to read minds based solely on a person's skin color, gender, or sexual preference. Then, they brand people as racist, sexist, homophobic, etc. without ever knowing them, which allows them to look away, justify, or even encourage others to spread hatred and violence, which are the very things they accuse the so-called oppressors of doing. Social justice adherents end up becoming what they apparently hate: advocates for racism, sexism, segregation, discrimination, and bigotry. They've convinced themselves they're the solution when they are most certainly the problem. They purposefully disseminate division and deconstruction to destroy our culture and its institutions, including the church. The utopian goal is to remake all of society in the image of a social justice activist.

In the end, the SJM is threatening to do in evangelical churches exactly what the Galatian heresy did 2000 years ago. It twists the Scriptures. It mixes faith with works. It continues and even advances through the fear of what people will think about us and do to us. It bewitches Christian leaders who should know better than to compromise the gospel with unbiblical ideology, and it punishes one group of people simply for not being a member of a different group of people. This is the Galatian heresy in twenty-first century dress. It is having the same effect now because like the Galatian heresy, the SJM is a distortion of the gospel. That is why Christians all over the world must never ignore it, embrace it, learn from it, integrate it with Christianity, or use it to analyze anything.

Instead, we must respond as Paul did to this heresy and to Peter's compromise: we must be the opposition with all the truth and love that God supplies. We must make every effort to guard the gospel as well as our Jesus-achieved, Spirit-produced unity, which always includes defending the truth against false teaching and those who propagate it. We must work to destroy this Godassaulting delusion (2 Cor 10:3–5). In the ugly, satanic face of to-day's SJM, faithful Christians everywhere, and especially our leaders, have no other choice but to stand.

STUDY QUESTIONS

1. Read Colossians 2:8 and 1 Timothy 6:20–21. How should Christians respond to ideologies coming from outside the Bible with no basis in biblical teachings?

2. Read Romans 16:17–20 and Titus 3:10–11. How are Christians supposed to think about and respond to people who cause divisions between Christians?

3. How do you think the evangelical church is doing in response to the SJM based on what you just read from the four sets of passages mentioned above? Please explain your answer.

PART 3

WHAT CAN CHRISTIANS DO TO STAND AGAINST THE SOCIAL JUSTICE MOVEMENT?

AN OASIS IN OUR LOST AND DYING WORLD

Throughout this book, I have tried to show that the Social Justice Movement (SJM) should not be treated like a friend or a mentor to the church of Jesus Christ. It is in no way part of Christianity's in-house debates. It is not only false and incompatible with Christianity; the SJM is anti-Christian. Other than platitudes about justice and caring about people—ideas that can only truly come from a theistic worldview anyway—social justice ideology is based on concepts from a completely different worldview than the one we are given in the Bible. Christians should never try to find common ground with the SJM or integrate it with the Bible. We should flee from it and fight against it.

The SJM is a counterfeit of the truth like the Galatian heresy was in Paul's day. I made this case in Parts 1 and 2 by showing that when the SJM redefines justice it not only distorts true justice, but it creates a different gospel. Like the experience of the Galatian churches, the different gospel of the SJM is devastating the unity Christians already have in Christ and in his church. Like the Galatian heresy, if the SJM stays in any group of Christians, it will not only create factions and two levels of Christians, the woke and the non-woke, but these two groups will become rivals unless the truth overcomes and unites. Church leaders who followed this failed strategy are appropriately and predictably reaping the bitter fruit they sowed with social justice seeds as their numbers plummet and members flee to churches faithful to the gospel.

Christian leaders should never be dupes for false doctrine like Peter and Barnabas were in Galatia (Gal 2:11–14). If they are going to be woke, they should wake up to the fact that the social justice counterfeit substitutes the truth for a lie and fractures the church Jesus united with his blood (Eph 2:13-15). While it pretends to be about things Christians should support, the SJM is really the latest in a long line of deadly attacks on the gospel that the true church has fought against since the days of the apostles. The scary part is, this is the fastest-growing anti-Christian religious movement to imbed itself in the culture and in the church in my lifetime. Tragically, the last time something similar to this happened was the Social Gospel Movement of the early twentieth century, which gave us the apostate wasteland of the mainline denominations. Hence, the title of this book, *Stand*. Faithful Christians who love the truth, who love the gospel, and who will never go woke because we love all our neighbors—we must stand against social justice ideology and do so with all our might. Paul was intolerant of every attack on Christ and the truth of the gospel, so we too must "stand firm" (Gal 5:1) against this racist, sexist, intolerant, bigoted cult that won't help anyone and can't save a single soul. As with all anti-Christian ideologies, the test is, will you submit to it through compromise or integration, or will you stand against it?

If Galatians is a paradigm for understanding the heresy of the SJM, then it also has the help we need to understand how Christians should respond. God's prescription for how to answer the SJM begins in Galatians 4. To churches filled with a false gospel thanks to false Christians and those who were deceived by their lies, Paul wrote,

> When you did not know God, you were enslaved to those that by nature are not gods. But now that you have come to know God, or rather to be known by God, how can you turn back again to the weak and worthless elementary principles of the world, whose slaves you want to be once more? (vv. 8-9)

These "elementary principles" are called "not gods" who enslave people. They are the rulers, the authorities, the cosmic powers over this present darkness, the spiritual forces of evil in the heavenly places (Eph 6:12) that originate and propagate false doctrine through the people they enslave (see 1 Tim 4:1-2, 2 Tim

2:25-26).[1] This same line of argument returns later on in Galatians, "You were running well. Who hindered you from obeying the truth? This persuasion is not from him who calls you" (Gal 5:7-8). If religious teaching is not from the God "who calls you," it ultimately comes from demonic forces, which are the source of every counterfeit-gospel movement, including the SJM.

This means our very first response should not be anger, disgust, or pity (though each is certainly appropriate), but it should be prayer. This battle is ultimately with beings in the invisible realm so our weapons must do damage there (2 Cor 10:3-4, Eph 6:10-18). We don't have the power or the wisdom to overcome the SJM within our circle of family and friends, let alone in our culture—only the triune God does! We may go through some terrible times of suffering, as I know some already have thanks to the infiltration of social justice ideology into their lives, so we must pray. Pray for your family members, especially the most susceptible. Pray for your friends. Pray for your country. Pray for your schools and school boards. Pray for your colleges and universities. Pray for the people in every branch of your local, state, and federal governments. Pray for the churches where you live and around the world. Pray that God would open your society's eyes both to the lies of the SJM and to the truth of the gospel.

Second, because these are demonic dogmas, we should expose them, warning people of the danger they are in if they embrace these lies, and encouraging all people, everywhere to give themselves to the truth instead. In response to the defection of some Galatian Christians from the truth, Paul unmasks the error by saying, "You observe days and months and seasons and years! I am afraid I may have labored over you in vain" (Gal 4:10-11) and later he alerts people that if the false teaching isn't stopped the result will be, "You are severed from Christ, you who would be justified by the law; you have fallen away from grace" (Gal 5:4). Paul is exposing the lies by contrasting what he taught with the false teaching the Galatians were tempted to believe. Throughout

---

[1] See Clint E. Arnold, *The Colossian Syncretism* (Grand Rapids: Baker Books, 1996).

the letter, the clear divide is not hard to see. Galatians has multiple arguments from many different angles that all show the contrast between truth and error. We must all do the same with today's SJM. Not only are Christians to "Take no part in the unfruitful works of darkness," but God also demands that we "expose them" (Eph 5:11).

Now, we cannot just be against social justice lies; we must be advocates for the truth it attacks as well. Both are essential! If we do not firmly love the truth, the world with its dominant influences will break us. If we unwaveringly love the truth, the Lord will be a hammer in our souls that will break the world. Why? Because Christianity is true and it's better! It is a healthier and more hopeful understanding of life than the one offered by the SJM. So, we give people the gospel no matter what: that all people were created by God, that all have sinned against him and exist with the sentence of eternal death hanging over their heads every second of every day (John 3:36; Rom 3:23, 6:23). However, that same God, out of his mercy and compassion for sinners, gave Jesus up to death as a substitute, and then he rose from the dead (John 3:14-16, Titus 3:3-7). God will grant total and complete forgiveness to all who will give their lives to Jesus, turning from their rebellion and trusting in him and him alone to save them from the eternal penalty they deserve for all of their sins (Acts 11:18, Eph 2:8). Why do we say this to people? Why do we call anyone and everyone to come to Christ and be saved (John 3:17-18, 36; Acts 17:30-31, Rom 10:9-13)? Because the truth will set them free from demonic ideas like the SJM (John 8:31-32) and because changed people can change other people. Together, supernaturally changed people can change society. It's happened before in world history and it can happen again.

Third, let's make sure our commitment to Jesus is seen in how we treat people, especially those who disagree with us because "in Christ Jesus neither circumcision nor uncircumcision counts for anything, but only faith working through love" (Gal 5:6). Our love for Jesus must be seen in our love for people because "the whole law is fulfilled in one word: 'You shall love your neighbor as yourself'" (Gal 5:13-14). The gospel frees us from the selfish, self-centered tendencies promoted by the SJM, empowering us to serve other people, doing what's best for them, and loving them as the Lord loves us (John 13:34–35). Now, in saying this, Christians must be very careful here. Dishonest people will seek to use our good desire to love people to manipulate us into advancing their agenda. Loving your neighbor has become the slogan used to promote error, accept the ideology, and even encourage blatantly sinful behavior. This can be manipulated to advance whatever the SJM wants. We must be on guard against this and not give up any ground. True love for our neighbors is doing everything possible to decelerate, demoralize, deconstruct, and destroy this demonic ideology in our schools, our jobs, our affinity groups, our churches, and anywhere else it rears its ugly head in our lives.

Love isn't icing on the cake of Christianity; it *is* Christianity! Let's be people who don't break off relationships (as far as that depends on us, according to Romans 12:16–21), but who forgive instead (Col 3:12–14). 1 Corinthians 16:14 makes our responsibility clear when it says, "let everything you do be done in love," including how you respond to the SJM with your family and friends as well as online. I recently heard former social justice warriors describe why they left the movement. Much of it had to do with how truly unloving the movement is.[2] The SJM has created an unloving, pharisaical cult of whiney babies that fight imaginary bogeymen while remaining largely silent about the greatest social evils in our day, like "black-on-black" crime, modern slavery, ethnic cleansing (which is actual racism), religious persecution, genocide, human trafficking, socialism, and abortion. What a substantial opportunity we have as the followers

---

[2] Keri Smith, "On Leaving the SJW Cult and Finding Myself," *Medium*, May 13, 2017, accessed September 18, 2021, https://medium.com/unsafe-space/on-leaving-the-sjw-cult-and-finding-myself-1a6769b2f1ff; Unsafe Spaces, "[Deprogramed] Monique Duson," *YouTube*, September 17, 2020, accessed September 3, 2021, https://www.youtube.com/watch?v=JG4yN-RfrOEQ; The Daily Wire, "From Unhappy Liberal to Hopeful Conservative: Amala Ekpunobi," *YouTube*, July 2, 2021, accessed September 6, 2022, https://www.youtube.com/watch?v=mZze_ZoWsOw.

Jesus, the King of Love, whose love for us can cause us to love people out of this hate-filled movement. If loving people means doing what's best for them, then it is love to fight an ideology that promotes hatred and division, that perpetuates racism, sexism, class warfare, and a whole host of ideas that have destroyed millions.

Biblical justice is true social justice and there's a long history of Christians rejecting the SJM while adorning the gospel with their love and good works (Titus 2:7, 10; Heb 10:24).[3] Christians should be, as many have been, at the forefront of fighting poverty, hunger, lack of health care, crime, abortion, poor education, and injustice, both in America and around the world. In seven short years, the church I get to pastor has by God's grace worked to combat many of those things and will continue to do so as we are always looking for ways to love more people. We're doing our small part as a fairly new church turnaround to stand and fight against injustice through love, not through embracing demonic ideas that propagate fear, guilt, envy, hatred, shame, greed, brutality, pride, and division.

Love is the motivation for this book—love for those who are bewitched by the SJM (Gal 3:1), those who are being tempted by it, those who have come to people like me with tears spilling out of their eyes over these issues, those who have lost their friends, their small group, their church, or their jobs in this struggle, those who no longer trust leaders they once greatly revered, and love for a country that's sprinting off a cliff to its own destruction while blindfolded by the SJM. This book is about love for people like one young woman who told me after church one Sunday that her family disowned her for rejecting the SJM. Her job and school are also overrun by the SJM, but our church was the only place

---

[3] See Alvin J. Schmidt, *Under the Influence: How Christianity Transformed Civilization* (Grand Rapids, MI: Zondervan, 2001); Vincent Carrol and David Shiflett, *Christianity on Trial: Arguments Against Anti-Religious Bigotry* (New York: Encounter Books, 2001); D. James Kennedy, *What if Jesus Had Never Been Born? The Positive Impact of Christianity in History* (Nashville, TN: Thomas Nelson, 2001); Jeremiah J. Johnston, *Unimaginable: What Our World Would Be Like Without Christianity* (Grand Rapids, MI: Baker, 2017).

in her life where she was safe. Love should be how we respond to those ensnared by the SJM, and when we do, we will be an oasis in the desert of our lost, angry, empty, and dying world.

STUDY QUESTIONS

1. Using the paradigm, God, sin, Jesus, response, write out a brief gospel presentation.

2. Read Galatians 5:7–10. Why is it so wrong to run people away from Christianity according to these verses? How does this relate to the SJM in the church?

3. List as many ways as you can to love those you know who are bewitched by the SJM in tangible ways.

THE BEWITCHING IS REAL

Building on the end of the previous chapter, the fourth response to the SJM and those deceived by its lies should never be hatred because "if you bite and devour one another, watch out that you are not consumed by one another" (Gal 5:15). In our fury and utter intolerance for false teaching, we should never let that spill over into unloving acts towards people in the SJM. This includes Christians caught up in it, and even Christian leaders who should know better. The SJM is based on atheistic philosophy that wants nothing to do with God. Why Christian leaders try to integrate it with Christianity and platform advocates for it just baffles me. It doesn't believe the best about people. It doesn't choose to trust people. It doesn't give anyone the benefit of the doubt. It doesn't bring people together despite their differences. It is not God's work done God's way as he declared in his Word. While all of that is true, none of it justifies hatred.

The SJM believes the worst, projects its bigotry on others, and offers no forgiveness. It actually endorses the activity in Galatians 5:15. Any movement that does this has Satan, "the father of lies" (John 8:44), as its ultimate source. It promotes the same hatred for people that he has always had. Like snakebites, social justice speech poisons people against each other. Like lions with their prey, social justice tears people to pieces. The results of the SJM are paralleled in "the works of the flesh," which are "sexual immorality, impurity, sensuality, idolatry, sorcery, enmity, strife, jealousy, fits of anger, rivalries, dissensions, divisions, envy, drunkenness, orgies, and things like these" (vv. 19-21). These are not diseases, quirks of personality, ethnicity, nationality, upbringing, or environment. These are all sins against God and other people, and almost all of them find official encouragement in the SJM.

The first three on the list, "sexual immorality, impurity, sensuality," are *sexual sins*. These are the opposite of love for God and other people (Rom 1:26–27, 1 Cor 6:9–11). Sexual activity outside of marriage between opposite gender spouses, as well as any desires or activities that cause a tender, innocent, unseared conscience to feel dirty are condemned with the first two words. The third word, *sensuality*, is sexual immorality and impurity without restraint. It is the celebration of debauchery without shame or concern for how others will be impacted. As works of the flesh, they are the epitome of love for self, something that is never seen positively in the Bible (see 2 Tim 3:1–2). With what we have seen so far in the SJM, there should be no surprise that it seeks to normalize sexual deviancy.[1] Movements like this try to deconstruct the nuclear family because the family unit offers a nearly impenetrable wall of protection from losing our identity and our values to movements like this.

The next two, "idolatry and sorcery," are *spiritual sins*. These are the opposite of love for God in that they reject him while giving allegiance to demons and their ideas. Predictably, the founders of one particularly influential and affluent organization, Black Lives Matter, practice the Yoruba religion, which includes idolatry, sorcery, and invoking help from "the dead" (demons disguising themselves as once-living-now-deceased people) and other entities. That's not slander. I've read and heard them say as much.[2] The same is true for much of feminism, which not only includes the normalizing of sexual deviancy, but also includes involvement in New Age and occult practices like the worship of female deities. Why Christians and Christian leaders think the

---

[1] No Author, "Black Lives Matter … What We Believe," *University of Central Arkansas*, unknown, accessed January 17, 2021, https://uca.edu/training/files/2020/09/black-Lives-Matter-Handout.pdf. For the full text of this document, see appendix 2.

[2] Hebah Farrag, "The Fight for Black Lives is a Spiritual Movement," Berkeley Center for Religion, Peace & World Affairs, June 9, 2020, accessed January 17, 2022, https://berkleycenter.georgetown.edu/respsonses/the-fight-for-black-lives-is-a-spiritual-movement. Listen to BLM leaders explain their occult views on The Hamilton Corner, "BLM founders are 'trained Marxists' and they are trained in other things too," *YouTube*, August 18, 2020, accessed August 31, 2020, https://www.youtube.com/watch?v=BuATODASSsQ.

THE BEWITCHING IS REAL

right move to reach lost people is to integrate the SJM with Christianity is truly horrifying.

The next eight sins on the list are *social sins*, "enmity, strife, jealousy, fits of anger, rivalries, dissensions, divisions, envy" (vv. 20–21). These evils destroy human relationships and when inflamed have destroyed people, neighborhoods, cities, entire ethnicities, and even civilizations. All of it is the opposite of loving God and loving people. It is self-centeredness taken to such an extreme that the result is actual harm done to other people. *Enmity* is a hostility that has settled down and lives securely in someone's heart. *Strife* separates people and energizes tension between them. *Jealousy* is resentment that comes from other people having what you think you deserve. *Fits of anger* refers to outbursts of unrestrained fury. The word translated "rivalries" has to do with seeing other people as your enemy and harming them to get what you want if necessary. The result of all this is "dissensions and factions" as people are separated into groups, some to love and others to hate. *Envy* is extreme, heart-dominating jealousy. It is a desire to destroy people because of and/or to get what they have. The same word is used in Matthew 27:18 to describe the diabolical attitude that motivated the religious leaders to plot the murder of Jesus. They had become so bitter towards him that they wanted him dead for the negative impact he had on their influence in Israel.

Finally, the last two words on the list are *self-indulgent sins*. *Drunkenness* includes drinking parties, regularly "getting wasted," and what people call alcoholism and drug addiction today. This word refers to a lack of self-control that leads to the overindulgence of any substance (even good ones like food). As an aside, it is quite patronizing to call these diseases instead of sins. It robs people of the freedom that comes from taking responsibility for their sinful behavior, admitting how self-centered it is, and recognizing the damage it causes the people who love them. The final word, "orgies," is better translated "wild parties."[3] It represents the lifestyle of a "partier" that can degenerate into further and further reveling, decadence, hedonism, carousing, and debauchery.

When each "work of the flesh" is considered, there is not one that the SJM consistently discourages and most of it is encouraged. That is because the movement is anti-Christ. What it teaches does not come from the Holy Spirit as it contradicts what he ensured was written in the Bible (2 Pet 1:19–21). We should not allow ourselves to be conformed to the anti-God world (Rom 12:2) that is fueling movements marked by the sinful behavior in Galatians 5:19–21. We must not be people who indulge these "works of the flesh," who come across as conceited by making it a habit of "provoking one another, [or] envying one another" (Gal 5:26). Christians should abominate all the activity on this list, and any movement that encourages or engages in it. This list should never be celebrated, excused, or seen as a viable option for getting one's goals achieved. This sinful, arrogant, vicious, anti-social, demonic behavior will never bring about justice. It will receive God's justice one day, however.

Why is this so important for Christians to see? The end of Galatians 5:21 says, "I warn you, as I warned you before, that those who do such things will not inherit the kingdom of God." That is why the SJM is anti-Christ. Nothing described in the paragraphs above can promote, establish, or help anyone enter the kingdom of God. Individual lives and movements marked by and encouraging "the works of the flesh," are "earthly, unspiritual, demonic" (Jas 3:15). The proof that the SJM is a demon-inspired movement that destroys what it touches in regards to ethnicity, gender, and sexuality is verified in the kinds of lives it produces, promotes, excuses, and defends. It is not Christian, so why in the world would Christians, especially Christian leaders, justify staying silent about it or try to integrate a movement that

---

[3] "The plural form is again used, with 'wild parties' (NLT) perhaps catching the idea fairly well (NIV and ESV "orgies" is too specifically sexual)" (Douglas J. Moo, *Galatians*, BECNT [Grand Rapids, MI: Baker Academic, 2013], 361).

produces Galatians 5:19-21 with the transnational movement Jesus started based on divine truth and sacrificial love? The confusion, cowardice and bewitching going on today is very real.

The fifth response Christians should have to the SJM is we must become a counter-culture marked by "love, joy, peace, patience, kindness, goodness, faithfulness, gentleness, [and] self-control" (Gal 5:22-23). These nine characteristics are much more than personal character qualities. They are community virtues that are based on God's character, lived out by Jesus, and produced in gatherings of Spirit-controlled Christians. For Americans, we must accept that with our nation spiraling further and further into God's judgment[4] (see Rom 1:18-32), it will more fully embrace godless ideologies like the SJM. Among many other things, that means we may soon be living like no other Christians in American history, that is, not only outside of the mainstream, but as a persecuted minority. Now, while that is not ideal, Jesus counsels his followers about this reality with

Blessed are those who are persecuted for righteousness' sake, for theirs is the kingdom of heaven. Blessed are you when others revile you and persecute you and utter all kinds of evil against you falsely on My account. Rejoice and be glad, for your reward is great in heaven, for so they persecuted the prophets who were before you. (Matt 5:10-12)

We should see it as an honor to be "not of this world" (John 17:14). It is best to be a counter-culture to a world under the judgment of Romans 1:24-28 and marked by the behavior of Romans 1:29-32 and Galatians 5:19-21. Make sure your kids know this too, that it is good to be different because it means we belong to Jesus and not to a world at war with him. As people filled with the Spirit, let's be a refuge from the fear and lies of our society.

---

[4] I preached through Habakkuk starting in January of 2021 where I helped Christians understand from the Bible how to live in this increasingly obvious reality. You can find the series at redeemeraz.org or in the playlists on the YouTube page for Redeemer Bible Church AZ.

Let's be a parallel universe where Christ and his truth reign. Let's be a community of saved people, transformed by the gospel, who *love* all people instead of hating any of them, no matter how hostile they are to us. Let's be marked by *joy* instead of depression over the state of our world, knowing that regardless of what happens here, Jesus is better than anything the world has to offer and he wins in the end (and we along with him!). Let's be at *peace* with all people, even when interpersonal strife seems justified because the God of the universe made peace with us (Rom 5:10–11, 2 Cor 5:18–20). Now, in saying that, Christians are certainly at war with false teaching and false teachers and we must dismantle both with everything we have (2 Cor 10:3–5). However, we must show grace and love towards the people we interact with daily, even if they're at war with us because they never stop being our mission field.

Let's be a people who are *patient*, not short-tempered or irritable, even with the most difficult social justice warriors we know. Patience is the way God treats us, right? Let's also be *kind*, a people marked by grace, not harshness or arrogance, but forgiving others as God forgave us (Eph 4:32, Col 3:13). Christians should be marked by what is *good*. We must be people controlled by the Bible, what it commands, what it forbids, and the life it encourages. This is in contrast to being controlled by our feelings, or by an ideology like the SJM that at its core is unbiblical, anti-God, and therefore, evil. Let's be a *faithful* people who are worthy of trust, like our Lord (1 Thess 5:24), instead of being those who are not dependable, who can't be trusted, and whose word is always questioned.

We may not think it will be effective, but we should also be *gentle*, meaning considerate and compassionate, putting ourselves in other people's shoes and caring about them, rather than being selfish, indifferent, or hardhearted. This, by the way, does not mean embracing the SJM, which promotes and defends doctrinal and practical evil. It means being on the front lines of fighting real injustice, as defined by the Bible, wherever we can, just as it says in Galatians 6:10, "as we have opportunity, let us do good to everyone, and especially to those who are of the household of faith." Finally, let's be a community of people who have *self-control*, who are disciplined, not tossed back and forth by every teaching that comes from our culture and every desire that comes into our heads (Eph 4:14). Let's be rooted, established, and unwavering in the truth (Col 2:6-7). We cannot let the world's hatred make us forget who we are or how God expects us to respond to people who see us as their enemies. We must never hate them back or treat them the way they treat us. Instead, we should love them and think of practical ways to treat them well without ever compromising the truth (Matt 5:38-48).

STUDY QUESTIONS

1. Why do you think so many Christians, including Christian leaders, are embracing the ideology and objectives of the SJM when it is so obviously anti-Christ?

2. What would our witness be like if churches and other Christian gatherings were oases in the desert of real life?

3. Read Matthew 5:10-12, 2 Timothy 3:11-12, and 1 Peter 4:12-16. What would our lives be like if we really believed the statements in these verses?

HAVING A STEEL SPINE

Galatians has more responses for faithful Christians in the face of false gospel crusades like the SJM. Sixth, we should, "Bear one another's burdens, and so fulfill the law of Christ" (Gal 6:2). We need to get together more with other Christians. We must attack the tendency many of us have to isolate in our homes, in front of our screens, insulated from everything we do not like about twenty-first century life, including the SJM. Rather, we need to be with one another more, giving thought to how we can "stir up one another to love and good works" (Heb 10:24–25). We must put aside our petty differences, forgive each other often, have each other's back, and give tangible help to one another as we all trudge through these dark days together. Our loyalty to and care for each other will be what helps us "fulfill the law of Christ," which refers to the command Jesus gave to love each other as He has loved us (John 13:34).

Sadly, some people are dealing with the SJM alone, but when we resist isolation, declutter our schedules, and prioritize getting together with other Christians, we will find courage and support. We need to talk to other Christians so they can get to know us, minister to us, and pray for us, and so we can do the same for them. Going back to the beginning of Chapter Nine, we need to do all that praying with each other. We also need to get informed about the SJM. We should read, listen to resources, and watch videos (like the many listed in appendix 1) with our brothers and sisters so we can discuss them with one another and grow together. We need churches and people across theological spectrums to work together too. The days of churches seeing each other as competition should have never started and has needed to end for decades. Knowing other ministries are united with you can be a tremendous encouragement to press on. We cannot let our secondary differences make us enemies any longer because we all need to fight the real enemy of the SJM. We must band together as a testimony to the world that we belong to Jesus (John 17:20-26). The spiritual attack being provoked by the SJM is more than theological. It's also a political and moral attack, so digesting content about the founding of countries like America, the Judeo-Christian ideals that undergird western society, and so on—all of that will help protect one another (especially our children!) in the days ahead.

Parents, you have a bigger job than just personal enrichment on these issues. You must push hard against the culture or it will swallow your kids. You have to take an active role in teaching them biblical truth, helping them see all of life as a response to God's existence and his care, and training them in how to evaluate right vs. wrong as well as pleasure vs. joy based on God's truth. If you fail to disciple your kids, if you give them over uncritically or unwittingly to the world and its values, it is all too happy to disciple your kids for you, which unfortunately includes where you send your kids to school. Though every school is different, the days of public schools being neutral in the culture war are increasingly coming to an end. We are in a battle between the kingdom of darkness and the kingdom of Christ where both sides are evangelistically trying to flip people's allegiances from one side to the other. Our commitments to Jesus, the content of Christianity, the Bible known and memorized, and our common history will protect our kids and keep us sane and united, especially if things get worse.

Seventh, we respond to the SJM by remembering, with deep humility and gratitude, that if it wasn't for God's grace, we'd embrace this or some other heresy too: "Keep watch on yourself, lest you too be tempted. . . . If anyone thinks he is something, when he is nothing, he deceives himself" (Gal 6:1b, 3). What we know about the SJM should never breed in us a sense of superiority. We should never think we are better than those who embrace the SJM, even the most brainwashed among them. We cannot take credit for anything we understand about God or the world he made. We need to be humble and grateful, and let that reality keep us from becoming arrogant towards those who are blind and lost (Luke 19:10, 2 Cor 4:4). We must also continue to hate false teaching and defend the truth against false teachers, confronting error with gentleness, respect, grace, wisdom, and kindness (Col 4:5–6, 2 Tim 2:24–26, 1 Pet 3:15). That might not get a lot of clicks, likes, or followers on social media, but life is NOT about "doing to others as they would do unto you." It's about doing to others as God has done to you, even on Twitter! He was gracious and compassionate in your rebellion, right? He didn't demean you as an idiot, laugh at you, or enjoy the thought of you suffering for your sins against him, right? He was merciful, so we need to be the same towards those who are in rebellion against the reality he created and the Son that he loves. This is not a distraction from evangelism; it is evangelism!

Eighth, we should not be afraid of the SJM. "It is those who want to make a good showing in the flesh who would force you to be circumcised, and only in order that they may not be persecuted for the cross of Christ" (Gal 6:12). The false teachers in Galatia were promoting false teaching because they were afraid of what some Jewish people would do to them. Out of pride and a desire to avoid persecution, they sought to impress people and they did so by throwing Gentiles under the theological bus. They wanted to be admired so they promoted false teaching. Then, the people who followed the false teaching became trophies for the false teachers to parade in front of the people they were trying to impress. However, they trampled the gospel and God's people to do so (Gal 6:13).

We should never try to curry favor with the world as a motivation. This has been a weakness of evangelicalism since its inception[1] and the peer pressure of the SJM, with its totalitarian tendencies, uses fear to change and control us as well as keep us divided. Fear and pride drive people to social media to virtue signal their support for the latest social justice campaign. In this whole discussion, let us never forget Galatians 1:10, "If I were still trying to please man, I would not be a servant of Christ." We either act as servants to people by fearing them and conforming

---

[1] For more on this assertion, see our *Redeemer Truth* interviews with Drs. Bill Roach (Episode 74) and Owen Strachan (Episode 78).

our actions to their desires, or we serve God by fearing him and doing what he wants regardless. We should never submit to the desire for people to like us, or be impressed with us by supporting a counterfeit message that assaults the gospel, damns people, and destroys churches. That's not evangelism; it's compromise.

The fear of man is a failing strategy to win people to the real Jesus. It will win them to a non-existent, social justice warrior Jesus, who is an example, a revolutionary, and a supposed liberator from earthly oppression, but he won't be their Savior or their Lord. You do not win the social justice crowd through accommodation or appeasement. You win them like everyone else is won to Christ, through confrontation with biblical truth done in humility, gentleness, respect, and love (Col 4:5-6, 1 Pet 3:15). They're going to attack and marginalize us as unloving and divisive for pointing out what the SJM is in contrast to the truth—so what! Let's make sure the way we carry ourselves while talking about the SJM doesn't give their slanderous smokescreens any merit.

Ninth, Christians should support people and ministries that are anti-woke, which includes ending support for ministries that have gone woke, since "the one who is taught the word [should] share all good things with the one who teaches" (Gal 6:6). In the most divisive, most influential, and most destructive attack on the evangelical church in recent decades, ministries and leaders who are standing firm in the battle should have our respect, our admiration, and our support. It's not easy taking on the woke mob. It's hard to be marginalized by colleagues. It's painful to have one's reputation tarnished in the community without actually sinning in any way. The thought of being canceled can be deeply intimidating. It hurts losing family and friends for the sake of exposing the social justice lies with biblical truth. If we are ever encouraged by the stand a leader takes, it is important to support him or her prayerfully with intercession, verbally with encouragement, and financially with donations. If we share in the spiritual blessings God has given to them, it is only right for them to share in our material blessings (Rom 15:27). This fortifies them to keep standing and it pleases the Lord (Heb 13:16).

Tenth and finally, we should resist the fear of suffering for the truth. As Paul put it, "I bear on my body the marks of Jesus" (Gal 6:17). Though the context of Hebrews 12:4 is struggling against personal sin, the sentiment behind it can apply here as well when it says, "In your struggle against sin you have not yet resisted to the point of shedding your blood." We're terrified to struggle against sinful ideologies like the SJM to the point of shedding people's opinions of us! The reason the ideology has made so many recent advances is that people refuse to fight it. Now, I'm not saying purposefully look for suffering, or build a brand by publicly attacking people you will be in heaven with one day. I am saying, let's pray for courage and against being afraid of suffering for "the truth [that] is in Jesus" (Eph 4:21).

Christian, can we admit that we're soft, and repent of that? We love comfort. We love peoples' good opinions of us. We have no connection to a Christianity where people we know well are imprisoned and even executed merely for being faithful Christians (see Acts 4-7). We live and let live. We don't want to rock the boat. We don't like upsetting the status quo. We leave that to others so we can live quiet lives, away from all controversy and strife. Now, while that's a good desire to have (1 Tim 2:1-2), Christianity is not a cult of self where Jesus exists to make you happy, safe, carefree, and to help you love yourself. That's paganism and our current idolatry of comfort encourages that paganism. When we're safe, relaxed, apathetic, distracted, and compliant we're the most praised and accepted people in our corrupt society, and we're the least like Jesus too. Remember, Jesus wasn't executed for being too calm, nuanced, too nice, and winsome.

What will happen when the fight against the gospel comes to you personally? What will happen when the attack is against everything you hold to be true and want to pass on to your kids and grandkids? What will happen when there are no safe spaces for you to hide? What do you do when the attack is real and could cause you harm professionally, financially, socially, and maybe even physically? Are you prepared to accept pain and loss to be faithful to Jesus? Am I? Now is the time to wrestle with these questions, while it is relatively safe to do so because how we respond in times of testing depends on the kind of people we are now becoming. We may live in a world of lies, but we do not have to live like they're true. In big ways and in small ways, we can and should resist, even if it's by walking away in moments where you're expected to speak up and support the lie. We greatly admire that solitary man in the crowd at a Hitler rally who did not raise his arm to hail him, right? Well, now is our time!

We can't fear being thought of negatively. We can't be afraid of the social media hordes coming to cancel us. We can't let what other people might think cause us to hesitate. We can't let anxiety keep us silent because friends and family might cut us out of their lives. We can't be terrified of being attacked. We must not fear the consequences of being faithful. We must live according to God's Word and the dictates of our consciences as long as our consciences are constrained by God's Word. If hatred, rejection, and suffering were normal for our Savior, we should expect nothing less for being faithful to him (John 15:18-20, 1 John 3:13). If fear makes us fold, the SJM wins, and we cannot afford to lose. Far too much is at stake.

We must have a steel spine in this brave new world because the fight against the real Jesus is coming for us whether we like it or not. If we just shut up and do what we're told, Christianity will be silenced. We must be a united army of men and women with zeal, who burn, who are consumed with pleasing God (2 Cor 5:10). We must endure every trial, push through all adversity, and remove everything in our lives that gets in the way of pleasing God (Mark 9:43-48). If God wills, we will suffer, labor, and toil to the point of exhaustion (1 Pet 3:13-17). We must "spend and be spent" (2 Cor 12:15), and do it again the next day, all so Jesus will be honored in our bodies "whether by life or by death" (Phil 1:20). Pastors, if you've been in agreement with the SJM, or if you've been silent while this heresy spreads all around you, please, repent or resign. Today's church needs leaders with the clarity and conviction of Paul, the courage of Peter, and the compassion of John. We cannot lose this fight or it could be another thousand years of darkness awaiting humanity on the other side.

Jesus did say "because you are not of the world, but I chose you out of the world, therefore the world hates you. Remember the word that I said to you: 'A servant is not greater than his master.' If they persecuted me, they will also persecute you" (John 15:19–20; see also John 16:33). Do we believe him on this? Then, why do we think that though they killed Jesus, the world will be kind to us and accept the truth just as long as we are winsome and don't offend them? People who have suffered know that God meets us in special ways in suffering. Such intimacy is so special that many find themselves thankful for the suffering because of the closeness they had with God at that time. Being accepted despite what we believe, as Christians in America have been for a couple hundred years now, is a historical irregularity that has gutted many of us of the courage and conviction we all need now.

Dear reader, may you and I resolve today, right now, to let our judgment day matter to us on this day (1 Cor 3:10–15, 2 Cor 5:10). Let's make sure that hearing "Well done" from our Lord (Matt 25:21) means more to us than any "Well done" we could ever hear from an unbelieving, anti-God, truth-ignoring, people-destroying culture. Sometimes standing means standing against a destructive ideology, like the SJM, and sometimes it means standing against our comfort-demanding, approval-loving hearts. However, we will never do the first until we are resolved to do the second. In these dark days, let's be determined, with all the strength, humility, and love that God supplies, to stand.

STUDY QUESTIONS

1. Read Colossians 4:5–6, 2 Timothy 2:24–26, 1 Peter 3:15. In your own words, summarize how Christians should interact with those who disagree with or are even hostile to their Savior.

2. Read John 15:18–20 and 1 John 3:13. How do you think living in countries with religious freedom has disconnected us

from this teaching and what do you think the overall effect of that disconnection is on the church where you live?

3. So, are you prepared to accept pain and loss to stand faithful to Jesus in these dark days? Now is the time to ask a question like this, as I said above. Therefore, I ask it here so you can wrestle through an answer.

CONCLUSION

One of the last times I ministered overseas, I taught church history to a group of pastors from 8a–5p every day for a week. It was a great time getting to know the twenty or so men who were all solid Christian brothers. It wasn't until the last day that I realized, as I looked out at the room during my closing lecture, they can relate to people all the way back to the very beginning of Christianity far better than I could. They suffer for being Christians just like most Christians have since the first century. Many of those men spent time in jail a few months after I left. Their crime? Being Christian pastors.

I saw the same thing in 2007 when I ministered in Ukraine and met an old pastor who suffered many years in prison under Communism for preaching Christ. Before that, in 2006, I saw the same thing in Egypt when a fake student compromised the school I was going to teach at and revealed its existence to the authorities so that we had to have class in a secret location. No pictures were allowed and every student used a phony name just in case I was interrogated at the airport. One student, who called himself Moses, told me his father tried to kill him when he found out that he had given his life to Jesus, but when our kids do that, we take them for ice cream! These experiences, not ours in America, are far closer to the historical norm for Christians.

I wonder, is there anything you believe that you're willing to die for? There is for each group of these non-American Christians, which is why, instead of submitting to tyranny, they stood firm against it. They illegally smuggle Bibles into their countries. They meet in underground churches in secret locations that the congregation only learns of an hour beforehand and no new people are allowed to attend unless a member in good standing vouches for them. They translate solid Christian books under the cover of darkness. They hide literature about Jesus in secret compartments in the walls and floors of their homes. They refuse to

89

let the tyranny they live under compete with Jesus as their Lord (Acts 4:18–20, 5:28–29) all because they rest in the truth that "the light shines in the darkness and the darkness has not overcome it" (John 1:5).

Reader, we do not get to choose when we live or what the attacks on the truth will be that come our way. I also do not get to choose what I see as a threat to protect God's people from and equip them to fight against. I see what I see regarding the SJM, that it is a pagan, godless, and merciless ideology. However, I took my thoughts to the Bible, logical argumentation, and history. Time after time, the great danger of this threat was overwhelmingly confirmed. If we are not willing to fight and suffer for standing against the SJM, Christianity is a nice idea, but it is not real to us. When it is, Christians take a stand. We stood against the Roman Empire. We stood against lions in the arena. We stood against heretical sects and false religions. We stood against persecutions, inquisitions, firing squads, and the stake. We stood against polytheism, atheism, fascism, Communism and so much more, and we are still here.

For all of that, many of our brothers and sisters were shunned, mocked, beaten, imprisoned, flogged, tortured, and killed, but the light has not even been phased (John 1:5). It keeps right on shining! Many are still standing today, right now, against socialism, Islam, ethnic cleansing, Hinduism, dictators, and other persecutors. They stand when everyone around them is giving up or giving in, even though it may cost them their lives and the lives of those they love most. For all that, we don't criticize them. We don't condemn them. We celebrate them. We bless their names and thank God for their examples for one reason only—they stand!

Just like compromise is contagious, courage is too. In these dark days, the question for us is the same question almost every Christian has had to ask throughout church history—will I stand? I pray that in big ways and small ways we will resist the lies of the SJM. Even if we stand alone, we are not alone. Not only will Jesus never forsake us (Matt 28:20, Heb 13:5), but there are brothers and sisters in our local churches, and all around the world who will support us too. We are stronger than we think. When we are united, we are strong. We must not go gentle into a social justice good night. We must rage against the dying of freedom's light (thank you Dylan Thomas!). Even if the whole world joins the SJM, I hope that Christians will defy the world and not even given an inch. Never forget that no matter what happens here, Jesus wins. Every expression of darkness has its day, and every single one is doomed to fail, including the SJM. We are in a battle we cannot be anything but victorious in. Let us be people of truth and love who are not afraid to challenge every attack on the gospel, who do so to honor God and for the eternal good of lost people even if they don't recognize it now (1 Pet 2:12). Let us be a people, with the Lord leading the way, who never give up, never give in, and never stop fighting for truth and for the common good until our faith becomes sight (1 John 3:2) and we hear "Well done" (Matt 25:21) because we chose on a day like today, never to bow the knee, but with all our hearts, to stand.

Am I a soldier of the cross,
A follower of the Lamb?
And shall I fear to own his cause,
Or blush to speak his name?

Must I be carry'd to the skies,
On flow'ry beds of ease;
While others fought to win the prize,
And sailed through bloody seas?

Are there no foes for me to face?
Must I not stem the flood?
Is this vile world a friend to grace,
To help me on to God?

Sure I must fight if I would reign,
Increase my courage, Lord!
I'll bear the toil, endure the pain,
Supported by Thy Word.

Thy saints in all this glorious war,
Shall conquer though they die;
They see the triumph from afar,
And seize it with their eye.

When that illustrious day shall rise,
And all Thy armies shine,
In robes of victory through the skies,
The glory shall be Thine.[1]

---

[1] Isaac Watts, *The Works of the Rev. Isaac Watts*, vol. 1 (Leeds; London: Edward Baines; William Baynes; Thomas Williams and Son; Thomas Hamilton; Josiah Conder, 1812), 438.

APPENDIX 1: RECOMMENDED RESOURCES

The following is a list of resources to understand and respond to the Social Justice Movement. Even though I do not agree with every word in every book, I list these here because they are particularly helpful for seeing why people all over the world must begin to stand against this heresy once and for all, especially Christians. The asterisk (*) refers to books that are not written by Christians. The check (√) is where you should start.

WEBSITES

American Reformer (americanreformer.org)
Colson Center for Christian Worldview
(http://www.colsoncenter.org)√

Defending Inerrancy
(https://defendinginerrancy.com/chicago-statements/)

Family Research Council (https://www.frc.org)

Heritage Action for America
(https://heritageaction.com/issues)

Joe Dallas (https://joedallas.com)

Just Thinking Ministries (https://justthinking.me)√

New Discourses (https://newdiscourses.com)√

Portland Fellowship
(https://www.portlandfellowship.com/clarity.php)

Sovereign Nations (https://sovereignnations.com)√

Stand to Reason (https://www.str.org)

The Council on Biblical Manhood and Womanhood
(https://cbmw.org)

The Danvers Statement (https://cbmw.org/about/danvers-statement)

The Nashville Statement (https://cbmw.org/nashville-statement)

The Social Justice Encyclopedia
(https://newdiscourses.com/translations-from-the-wokish/)

The Statement on Social Justice and the Gospel
(https://statementonsocialjustice.com)√

BOOKS: GENERAL

Alexander Solzhenitsyn. *The Gulag Archipelago*. 3 vols. Harper, 2007.√

Alisa Childers. *Another Gospel?* Tyndale, 2020.

Augustine. *The City of God*. Digireads.com, 2017.

Carl Trueman. *The Rise and Triumph of the Modern Self: Cultural Amnesia, Expressive Individualism, and the Road to Sexual Revolution*. Crossway, 2020.

D. A. Carson. *The Intolerance of Tolerance*. Eerdmans, 2012.

Dennis Prager. *Still the Best Hope: Why the World Needs American Values to Triumph*. Broadside, 2013.*√

Douglas Murray. *The Madness of Crowds: Gender, Race and Identity*. Bloomsbury, 2019.*

E. Calvin Beisner. *Social Justice vs. Biblical Justice: How Good Intentions Undermine Justice and Gospel*. GoodTrees, 2018.

Erwin Lutzer. *We Will Not Be Silenced: Responding with Courage to Our Culture's Assault on Christianity*. Harvest House, 2020.

Francis A. Shaeffer. *The Complete Works of Francis A. Schaeffer: A Christian Worldview*. Vol. 5, *A Christian View of the West*. Crossway, 1982.

Frank Dikotter. *The Cultural Revolution: A People's History 1962–1976*. Bloomsbury, 2016.*

Frank Dikotter. *The Tragedy of Liberation: A History of the Chinese Revolution 1945-1957*. Bloomsbury, 2013.*

Fyodor Dostoyevsky. *Demons*. Digireads.com, 2017.*

George Orwell. *Animal Farm and 1984*. Mariner, 2003.*

Iain Murray. *The Undercover Revolution: How Fiction Changed Britain*. Banner of Truth, 2009.

Igor Shafarevich. *The Socialist Phenomenon*. Gideon House, 2019.*

J. Gresham Machen. "The Present Situation in the Presbyterian Church." *Christianity Today* (May 1930): 5-7.

Jared Longshore. *By What Standard?: God's World...God's Rules*. Founders Press, 2020.

John Stonestreet and Brent Kunkle. A Practical Guide to Culture: Helping the Next Generation Navigate Today's World. David C. Cook, 2020.√

Josef Pieper. Abuse of Language, Abuse of Power. Ignatius, 1992.

Josh Buice. "Why is Social Justice the Biggest Threat to the Church in the Last One Hundred Years?" *Delivered By Grace*. April 4, 2019. Accessed December 21, 2021. https://g3min.org/social-justice-biggest-threat/.

Loung Ung. First They Killed My Father: A Daughter of Cambodia Remembers. Harper, 2006.*

Ludwig von Mises. *Marxism Unmasked: From Delusion to Destruction*. Ludwig von Mises Institute, 2010.*

Mark Coppenger. *A Christian View of Justice*. Broadman & Holman, 1983.

Mark Kramer (ed.). *The Black Book of Communism: Crimes, Terror, Repression*. Harvard, 1999.*

Michael Rectenwald. *Beyond Woke*. New English Review Press, 2020.*

Michael Rectenwald. *Springtime for Snowflakes: "Social Justice" and its Postmodern Parentage*. New English Review Press, 2018.*

Noelle Mering. *Awake, Not Woke: A Christian Response to the Cult of Progressive Ideology*. TAN Books, 2021.

Os Guinness. *Last Call for Liberty: How America's Genius for Freedom Has Become Its Greatest Threat*. IVP, 2018.

Os Guinness. *The Magna Carta of Humanity: Sinai's Revolutionary Faith and the Future of Freedom*. IVP, 2021.√

R. C. Sproul. *The Consequence of Ideas.* Crossway, 2009.√

Richard Pipes. *Communism: A History.* Modern Library, 2003.*

Robert Jay Lifton. *Thought Reform and the Psychology of Totalism: A Study of 'Brainwashing' in China.* Martino Fine Books, 2014.

Rod Dehrer. *Live Not By Lies.* Sentinel, 2020.√

Rodney Stark. *The Victory of Reason: How Christianity Led to Freedom, Capitalism, and Western Success.* Random House, 2006.

Ronald Nash. *Social Justice and the Christian Church.* Academic Renewal, 2002.

Ryszard Legutko. *The Demon in Democracy: Totalitarianism Temptations in Free Societies.* Encounter, 2018.*

Scott Allen. *A Toxic New Religion: Understanding the Postmodern, Neo-Marxist Faith that Seeks to Destroy the Judeo-Christian Culture of the West.* Disciple Nations Alliance, 2020.√

Scott Allen. *Why Social Justice Is Not Biblical Justice: An Urgent Appeal to Fellow Christians in a Time of Social Crisis.* Credo, 2020.√

W. Cleon Skousen. *The Naked Communist.* Izzard Ink Publishing, 2017.*

William Bennett. *America: The Last Best Hope* (One-Volume Edition). Thomas Nelson, 2019.*√

William J. Federer. *Socialism: The Real History from Plato to the Present.* Amerisearch, Inc., 2020.

William J. Federer. *Who is the King in America? And Who are the Counselors to the King?: An Overview of 6,000 Years of History & Why America is Unique.* Amerisearch, Inc., 2017.

BOOKS: FEMINISM

Abigail Dodds. *(A)Typical Woman: Free, Whole, and Called in Christ.* Crossway, 2019.

Alexander Strauch. *Men and Women, Equal Yet Different: A Brief Study of the Biblical Passages on Gender.* Lewis & Roth, 1999.√

Andreas J. Köstenberger. *God, Marriage, and Family: Rebuilding the Biblical Foundation.* Crossway, 2010.

Andreas J. Köstenberger. *God's Design for Man and Woman: A Biblical-Theological Survey.* Crossway, 2014.

Carolyn McCully. *Radical Womanhood: Feminine Faith in a Feminist World.* Moody, 2008.√

John Piper and Wayne Grudem. *Recovering Biblical Manhood and Womanhood: A Response to Evangelical Feminism.* Crossway, 2021.

Margaret Elizabeth Köstenberger. *Jesus and the Feminists: Who Do They Say That He Is?* Crossway, 2008.

Mary Kassian. *The Feminine Mistake.* Crossway, 2005.

Owen Strachan. *Reenchanting Humanity: A Theology of Mankind.* Mentor, 2019.

Owen Strachan and Gavin Peacock. *The Grand Design: Male and Female He Made Them.* Christian Focus, 2016.√

Sharon James. *God's Design for Women in an Age of Gender Confusion.* EP Books, 2019.

Stephen B. Clark. *Man and Woman in Christ: An Examination of the Roles of Men and Women in Light of Scripture and the Social Sciences.* Servant, 1980.

Wayne Grudem. *Evangelical Feminism and Biblical Truth: An Analysis of More Than 100 Disputed Questions.* Crossway, 2012.

Wayne Grudem. *Evangelical Feminism: A New Path to Liberalism?* Crossway, 2006.

BOOKS: LGBT

Abigail Shrier. *Irreversible Damage: The Transgender Craze Seducing Our Daughters.* Regnery, 2020.*

Adam T. Barr and Ron Citlau. *Compassion Without Compromise: How the Gospel Frees Us to Love Our Gay Friends Without Losing the Truth.* Bethany House, 2014.

Anne Paulk. *Restoring Sexual Identity: Hope for Women Who Struggle with Same-Sex Attraction.* Harvest House, 2003.

Becket Cook. *A Change of Affection: A Gay Man's Incredible Story of Redemption.* Thomas Nelson, 2019.

Deborah Soh. *The End of Gender: Debunking the Myths about Sex and Identity in Our Society.* Threshold, 2020.*

Denise Shick. *Understanding Gender Confusion: A Faith Based Perspective.* Createspace, 2014.

Denny Burk and Heath Lambert. *Transforming Homosexuality: What the Bible Says About Sexual Orientation and Change.* P&R, 2015.

Denny Burk. *What is the Meaning of Sex?* Crossway, 2013.

Gavin Peacock and Owen Strachan. *What Does the Bible Teach about Homosexuality?* Christian Focus, 2020.√

Gavin Peacock and Owen Strachan. *What Does the Bible Teach about Transgenderism?* Christian Focus, 2020.√

Helen Joyce. *Trans: When Ideology Meets Reality.* One World, 2021.*

J. Alan Branch. *Affirming God's Image: Addressing the Transgender Question with Science and Scripture.* Lexham, 2019.

J. Alan Branch. *Born This Way?: Homosexuality, Science, and the Scriptures.* Lexham, 2018.

J. Budziszewski. *On the Meaning of Sex.* Intercollegiate Studies Institute, 2014.

J.D. Unwin. *Sex and Culture.* CreateSpace Independent Publishing Platform, 1934.*

Janelle Hallman. *The Heart of Female Same-Sex Attraction: A Comprehensive Counseling Resource.* InterVarsity, 2008.

Jeanette Howard. *Out of Egypt: One Woman's Journey Away From Lesbianism.* Monarch, 2001.*

Joe Dallas. *Desires in Conflict: Hope for Men Who Struggle with Sexual Identity.* Harvest Houses, 2003.

Joe Dallas. *Speaking of Homosexuality: Discussing the Issues with Kindness and Clarity.* Baker Books, 2016.

Joe Dallas. *When Homosexuality Hits Home: What to Do When a Loved One Says, I'm Gay.* Harvest House, 2015.

Joe Dallas and Nancy Heche. *The Complete Christian Guide to Understanding Homosexuality: A Biblical and Compassionate Response to Same-Sex Attraction.* Harvest House, 2010.

Kevin DeYoung. *What Does the Bible Really Teach About Homosexuality?* Crossway, 2015.√

Nancy Pearcey. *Love Thy Body.* Baker Books, 2018.√

Robert Gagnon. *The Bible and Homosexual Practice*. Abingdon, 2002.

Rosaria Butterfield. *The Secret Thoughts of an Unlikely Convert: An English Professor's Journey into Christian Faith*. Crown & Covenant, 2012.

Ryan T. Anderson. *When Harry Became Sally: Responding to the Transgender Moment*. Encounter, 2018.√

Sharon James. *Gender Ideology: What Do Christians Need to Know?* Christian Focus, 2019.

Walt Heyer. *Trans Life Survivors*. Self-Published, 2018.

BOOKS: ETHNICITY

Babylon Bee. *The Babylon Bee Guide to Wokeness*. Salem, 2021.

Bradley A. U. Levinson. *Beyond Critique: Exploring Critical Social Theories and Education*. Taylor & Friends, 2015.*

Carol M. Swain and Christopher J. Schorr. *Black Eye for America: How Critical Race Theory is Burning Down the House*. Be The People Books, 2021.

Charles Pincourt with James Lindsay. *Counter Wokecraft: A Field Manual for Combatting the Woke in the University and Beyond*. New Discourses, 2021.*

Christopher Paslay. *A Parent's Guide to Critical Race Theory: Fighting CRT in Your Child's School*. Independently Published, 2021.

Daniel A. Farber and Suzanna Sherry. *Beyond All Reason: The Radical Assault on Truth in American Law*. Oxford University Press, 1997.*

Don Jordan and Michael Walsh. *White Cargo: The Forgotten History of Britain's White Slaves in America*. NYU Press, 2008.

Heather Mac Donald. *The Diversity Delusion: How Race and Gender Pandering Corrupt the University and Undermine Our Culture*. St. Martin's Press, 2018.*

Heather Mac Donald. *The War on Cops: How the New Attack on Law and Order Makes Everyone Less Safe*. Encounter Books, 2017.*

Helen Pluckrose and James Lindsay. *Cynical Theories: How Activist Scholarship Made Everything about Race, Gender, and Identity — And Why This Harms Everybody*. Pitchstone, 2020.*√

James Lindsay. *Race Marxism*. New Discourses, 2022.*

Jason Riley. *Please Stop Helping Us: How Liberals Make It Harder for Blacks to Succeed*. Encounter, 2016.*

Jeffrey Johnson. *What Every Christian Needs to Know about Social Justice*. Free Grace, 2021.

Jesse Lee Peterson. *From Rage to Responsibility: Black Conservative Jesse Lee Peterson and America Today*. Paragon, 2000.*

John McWhorter. *Woke Racism: How a New Religion Has Betrayed Black America*. Portfolio, 2021.*

Jon Harris. *Christianity and Social Justice: Religions in Conflict*. Reformation Zion, 2021.

Jon Harris. *Social Justice Goes to Church: The New Left in Modern American evangelicalism*. Ambassador, 2020.

Jonathan Isaac. *Why I Stand*. DW Books, 2022.

Larry Koger. *Black Slaveowners*. McFarland & Company, 2011.

Michael Hoffman. *They Were White and They Were Slaves: The Untold History of the Enslavement of Whites in Early America.* Independent History, 1993.

Noah Rothman. *Unjust: Social Justice and the Unmaking of America.* Gateway, 2019.*

Owen Strachan. *Christianity and Wokeness.* Salem Books, 2021.√

Randall L. Kennedy. "Racial Critiques of Legal Academia." *Harvard Law Review* 102 (1989): 1745–1819.*

Richard Caldwell. *A Biblical Answer for Racial Unity.* Kress, 2018.

Roger Scruton. *Fools, Frauds, and Firebrands: Thinkers of the New Left.* Bloomsbury, 2017.*

Shelby Steele. *Shame: How America's Past Sins Have Polarized Our Country.* Basic, 2016.*

Shelby Steele. *White Guilt: How Blacks and Whites Together Destroyed the Promise of the Civil Rights Era.* Harper, 2007.*

Thomas Sowell. *Discrimination and Disparities.* Basic, 2019.*

Thomas Sowell. *Economic Facts and Fallacies.* Basic, 2011.*

Thomas Sowell. *Intellectuals and Race.* Harper, 2007.*

Thomas Sowell. *The Quest for Cosmic Justice.* Free Press, 2001.*

Thomas Sowell. *The Vision of the Anointed: Self-congratulation as a Basis for Social Policy.* Basic, 2019.

Voddie Baucham, Jr. *Faultlines: The Social Justice Movement and evangelicalism's Looming Catastrophe.* Salem Books, 2021.√

Walter Williams. *Race & Economics: How Much Can Be Blamed on Discrimination?* Hoover Institute, 2011.

STAND: CHRISTIANITY VS. SOCIAL JUSTICE

VIDEOS

Albert Mohler. "Live Not by Lies: A Conversation with Author Rod Dreher about Moral Resistance in a Secular Age." *YouTube*. October 28, 2020.

Alisa Childers. "Race, Injustice, and the Gospel of Critical Race Theory, With Monique Duson — #72." *YouTube*. June 9, 2020.

Apologia Acts 17:17. "Francis Schaeffer - The Watershed of the evangelical World." *YouTube*. March 12, 2012.√

Ben Shapiro. "7 Reasons Why 'White Fragility' is the Worst Book Ever." *YouTube*. June 29, 2020.

Colson Center. "What Kind of People Will We Be? The Church and the Culture at a Crossroads." *YouTube*. January 14, 2022.√

Conversations That Matter. "A Social Justice Evangelical Vocabulary of Terms." *YouTube*. September 4, 2021.

Conversations That Matter. "Hebrew Scholar Refutes Keller, Platt, & Anyabwile." *YouTube*. October 8, 2021.√

Conversations That Matter. "Juneteenth Follow Up and Four Woke Church Tactics." *YouTube*. June 23, 2021.√

Conversations That Matter. "Preparing Young People for Social Justice." *YouTube*. March 23, 2022.

Conversations That Matter. "Responding to Christian Homosexuality Part 2." *YouTube*. January 11, 2022.√

Conversations That Matter. "Who's Funding the Evangelical Social Justice Movement?" *YouTube*. February 11, 2019.

Coral Ridge. "Biblical Justice vs. Social Justice | Voddie Baucham." *YouTube*. February 18, 2021.

Cordial Curiosity. "Explaining Critical Social Justice with James Lindsay | React & Explain." *YouTube*. April 2, 2020.

Disciple Nations Alliance. "A Pastor's Response to Unbiblical Justice with Pastor Jon Benzinger." *YouTube*. March 26, 2021.

Fixed Point Foundation. "Understanding Socialism, Marxism, & the Radical Left's Plan for America." *YouTube*. October 17, 2020.

Founders Ministries. "Cultural Marxism | Dr. Voddie Baucham." *YouTube*. February 21, 2019.

Founders Ministries. "Ethnic Gnosticism | Dr. Voddie Baucham." *YouTube*. March 28, 2019.

Founders Ministries. "God of Justice & Mercy | Jared Longshore, Tom Ascol, Virgil Walker, Darrell Harrison, Voddie Baucham." *YouTube*. April 29, 2021.

Founders Ministries. "TS&TT: Voddie Baucham | Fault Lines in American evangelicalism." *YouTube*. October 20, 2020.

Grace to You. "Session 9: Irreconcilable Views of Reconciliation (Voddie Baucham)." *YouTube*. January 9, 2020.√

Grace to You. "Social Justice and the Gospel, Part 1." *YouTube*. September 5, 2018.√

Just Thinking Podcast. "EP # 102 | 'Black Lives Matter?'" *YouTube*. June 28, 2021.√

Just Thinking Podcast. "EP # 103 | 'The Church of BLM.'" *YouTube*. June 29, 2021.

Just Thinking Podcast. "EP # 108 | Critical Race Theory." *YouTube*. February 4, 2021.√

Just Thinking Podcast. "Just Thinking Podcast | Whiteness." *YouTube.* July 15, 2019.√

New Discourses. "A Brief History of Identity Marxism." *YouTube.* December 1, 2021.

New Discourses. "Antonio Gramsci, Cultural Marxism, Wokeness, and Leninism 4.0." *YouTube.* January 21, 2021.

New Discourses. "Five Key Points to Understand About Critical Race Theory." *YouTube.* December 20, 2021.√

New Discourses. "Introducing Race Marxism." *YouTube.* February 15, 2022.

New Discourses. "NO! Critical Race Theory Does NOT Continue the Civil Rights Movement." *YouTube.* February 15, 2021.√

New Discourses. "Saying No to Critical Race Theory." *YouTube.* July 20, 2020.

New Discourses. "The Cult Dynamics of Wokeness." *YouTube.* June 22, 2020.

New Discourses. "The Truth About Critical Methods | James Lindsay." *YouTube.* March 19, 2020.

New Discourses. "Understanding Diversity, Equity, and Inclusion." *YouTube.* September 25, 2020.√

PragerU. "What Is Critical Race Theory?" *YouTube.* April 26, 2021.√

PragerU. "What Is Social Justice?" *YouTube.* March 24, 2014.√

PSU College Republicans. "Is Intersectionality a Religion?" *YouTube.* March 3, 2018.

Redeemer Bible Church. "Christianity & Wokeness | Dr. Owen Strachan | What Are the Major Claims of Wokeness?" Session 1–5. *YouTube.* October 5, 2020.√

Redeemer Bible Church AZ. "Ep 24 | Lust, Homosexuality, & Transgenderism | Redeeming Truth." *YouTube.* May 6, 2020.√

Redeemer Bible Church AZ. "Ep 28 | Race, Rage, Justice, #GeorgeFloyd and the Gospel | Redeeming Truth." *YouTube.* June 3, 2020.√

Redeemer Bible Church AZ. "Ep 45 | The Need for Courage | Redeeming Truth." *YouTube.* October 1, 2020.

Redeemer Bible Church AZ. "Ep 49 | Interviews on Social Justice | Redeeming Truth." *YouTube.* November 6, 2020.

Redeemer Bible Church AZ. "Ep 50 | Dialogues on Social Justice, Pt 1 w/ Prof. Craig Hawkins | Redeeming Truth." *YouTube.* November 13, 2020.√

Redeemer Bible Church AZ. "Ep 51 | Dialogues on Social Justice, Pt 2 w/ Darrell & Virgil from Just Thinking | Redeeming Truth." *YouTube.* November 20, 2020.√

Redeemer Bible Church AZ. "Ep 52 | Dialogues on Social Justice, Pt. 3 w/ Owen Strachan | Redeeming Truth." *YouTube.* November 27, 2020.√

Redeemer Bible Church AZ. "Ep 54 | Progressive Christianity & Social Justice: A Conversation w Alisa Childers | Redeeming Truth." *YouTube.* December 11, 2020.

Redeemer Bible Church AZ. "Ep 57 | Further Clarification on Social Justice w/ Craig Hawkins | Redeeming Truth." *YouTube.* January 1, 2021.√

Redeemer Bible Church AZ. "Ep 58 | Living in a Nation Under God's Judgment | Redeeming Truth." *YouTube*. January 22, 2021.

Redeemer Bible Church AZ. "Ep 74 | Detecting the Shift in Evangelicalism with Dr. William Roach | Redeeming Truth." *YouTube*. May 21, 2021.

Redeemer Bible Church AZ. "EP 78 | Having Courage in a Woke Culture | Redeeming Truth #OwenStrachan." *YouTube*. August 12, 2021.

Sovereign Nations. "Defining Social Justice | Dr. Voddie Baucham." *YouTube*. January 30, 2019.√

Sovereign Nations. "Diversity, Inclusion, Equity | James Lindsay." *YouTube*. October 27, 2020.√

Sovereign Nations. "Identity Politics & The Marxist Lie of White Privilege | Dr. Jordan B. Peterson." *YouTube*. January 30, 2019.

Sovereign Nations. "The Great Awokening Conference." *YouTube*. October 26, 2020.

Sovereign Nations. "Trojan Horse - Ep. 1: Deconstructing Communities | Peter Boghossian, James Lindsay." *YouTube*. August 9, 2019.√

Sovereign Nations. "The Trojan Horse - Ep. 2: Radical Subjectivity | Peter Boghossian, James Lindsay, Michael O'Fallon." *YouTube*. September 5, 2019.

Sovereign Nations. "The Trojan Horse Ep. 3: Critical Race Theory | James Lindsay, Michael O'Fallon." *YouTube*. October 11, 2019.

Sovereign Nations. "How Did This Happen? | Public Occurrences, Ep. 59." *YouTube*. January 13, 2022.

Stanmore Baptist Church. "Social Justice - 2019 Apologetics Conference with Dr James White (Session 3)." *YouTube*. October 26, 2019.

APPENDIX 2: WHAT BLACK LIVES MATTER BELIEVES

The following is a document the Black Lives Matter organization once had on their website entitled, "Black Lives Matter ... What We Believe." They removed it in September 2020 and up until the time this book was written it has not been reposted. It is here to show that the claims made about the SJM aren't fabricated or exaggerated. While they are but one of many social justice organizations, BLM is the most influential, and their beliefs and goals are not outside of the movement's mainstream. Here, in their own words, is what they believe:

Four years ago, what is now known as the Black Lives Matter Global Network began to organize. It started out as a chapter-based, member-led organization whose mission was to build local power and to intervene when violence was inflicted on Black communities by the state and vigilantes. In the years since, we've committed to struggling together and to imagining and creating a world free of anti-Blackness, where every Black person has the social, economic, and political power to thrive.

Black Lives Matter began as a call to action in response to state-sanctioned violence and anti-Black racism. Our intention from the very beginning was to connect Black people from all over the world who have a shared desire for justice to act together in their communities. The impetus for that commitment was, and still is, the rampant and deliberate violence inflicted on us by the state. Enraged by the death of Trayvon Martin and the subsequent acquittal of his killer, George Zimmerman, and inspired by the 31-day takeover of the Florida State Capitol by POWER U and the Dream Defenders, we took to the streets. A year later, we set out together on the Black Lives Matter Freedom Ride to Ferguson, in search of justice for Mike Brown and all of those who have been torn apart by state-sanctioned violence and anti-Black racism. Forever changed, we returned home and began building the infrastructure for the Black Lives Matter Global Network, which, even in its infancy, has become a political home for many.

Ferguson helped to catalyze a movement to which we've all helped give life. Organizers who call this network home have ousted anti-Black politicians, won critical legislation to benefit Black lives, and changed the terms of the debate on Blackness around the world. Through movement and relationship building, we have also helped catalyze other movements and shifted culture with an eye toward the dangerous impacts of anti-Blackness.

These are the results of our collective efforts.

The Black Lives Matter Global Network is as powerful as it is because of our membership, our partners, our supporters, our staff, and you. Our continued commitment to liberation for all Black people means we are continuing the work of our ancestors and fighting for our collective freedom because it is our duty.

Every day, we recommit to healing ourselves and each other, and to co-creating alongside comrades, allies, and family a culture where each person feels seen, heard, and supported.

We acknowledge, respect, and celebrate differences and commonalities.

We work vigorously for freedom and justice for Black people and, by extension, all people.

We intentionally build and nurture a beloved community that is bonded together through a beautiful struggle that is restorative, not depleting. We are unapologetically Black in our positioning. In affirming that Black Lives Matter, we need not qualify our position. To love and desire freedom and justice for ourselves is a prerequisite for wanting the same for others.

We see ourselves as part of the global Black family, and we are aware of the different ways we are impacted or privileged as Black people who exist in different parts of the world.

We are guided by the fact that all Black lives matter, regardless of actual or perceived sexual identity, gender identity, gender expression, economic status, ability, disability, religious beliefs or disbeliefs, immigration status, or location.

We make space for transgender brothers and sisters to participate and lead.

We are self-reflexive and do the work required to dismantle cisgender privilege and uplift Black trans folk, especially Black trans women who continue to be disproportionately impacted by trans-antagonistic violence.

We build a space that affirms Black women and is free from sexism, misogyny, and environments in which men are centered.

We practice empathy. We engage comrades with the intent to learn about and connect with their contexts.

We make our spaces family-friendly and enable parents to fully participate with their children.

We dismantle the patriarchal practice that requires mothers to work "double shifts" so that they can mother in private even as they participate in public justice work.

We disrupt the Western-prescribed nuclear family structure requirement by supporting each other as extended families and "villages" that collectively care for one another, especially our children, to the degree that mothers, parents, and children are comfortable.

We foster a queer-affirming network. When we gather, we do so with the intention of freeing ourselves from the tight grip of heteronormative thinking, or rather, the belief that all in the world are heterosexual (unless s/he or they disclose otherwise).

We cultivate an intergenerational and communal network free from ageism. We believe that all people, regardless of age, show up with the capacity to lead and learn.

We embody and practice justice, liberation, and peace in our engagements with one another.

For more helpful resources
that encourage, equip, and educate the church,
visit **www.G3Min.org**.